WRITERS AND THEIR WORK

ISOBEL ARMSTRONG
General Editor

PERCY BYSSHE SHELLEY

Reproduced by kind permission of Major R. P. Owen whose Devon family has owned it for more than 100 years.

PERCY BYSSHE SHELLEY
A portrait of Shelley (c.1810), attributed to Sir Thomas Lawrence.

PERCY BYSSHE SHELLEY

Paul Hamilton

NORTHCOTE

BRITISH COUNCIL

ATLANTIC
PUBLISHERS & DISTRIBUTORS (P) LTD

This edition is published by
ATLANTIC
PUBLISHERS & DISTRIBUTORS (P) LTD
7/22, Ansari Road, Darya Ganj, New Delhi-110 002
Tel: 40775252, 23273880, 23275880, 23280451; Fax: +91-11-23285873
E-mail: orders@atlanticbooks.com; Web: www.atlanticbooks.com

By arrangement with
Northcote House Publishers Ltd
Horndon House, Horndon, Tavistock, Devon, PL19 9NQ,
United Kingdom. (T)+44(0)1822 810066; (F)+44(0)1822 810034
(E) northcote.house@virgin.net and (W) www.northcotehouse.co.uk
The *Writers and their Work* series is published in association with the British Council.

First Indian Reprint 2010
First published in 2000 by Northcote House Publishers Ltd

ISBN 978-81-269-1293-3

British Library Cataloguing-in-Publication Data
A catalogue record for this book is available from the British Library

Typeset by PDQ Typesetting, Newcastle-under-Lyme
Printed in India at Nice Printing Press, A-33/3A, Site-IV,
Industrial Area, Sahibabad, Ghaziabad, U.P.

Contents

Acknowledgements

I would like to thank Isobel Armstrong for vigorously encouraging me to take on this project. Anne Janowitz, Catherine Maxwell, Michael Rossington, and Clair Wills very kindly found time to read it and make suggestions for which I am hugely grateful. Hilary Walford was a marvellous copy editor. Anyone working on Shelley in this country is immediately in debt to the late Geoffrey Matthews and his editorial successor, Kelvin Everest. Shelley is one of the most exacting poets to write about. My personal obligations are to Dan and Reeta for keeping me safely in 'the web of human things' while this adventure lasted.

Biographical Outline

1792 Percy Bysshe Shelley born in Field Place, Horsham, Sussex. His grandfather, Bysshe, acceded to a baronetcy in 1806, inherited by Percy's father, Timothy, in 1815.

1802–4 After private tutoring, goes to school at Syon House Academy, Isleworth.

1804–10 A schoolboy at Eton.

1808–10 Enjoys largely epistolary relationship with cousin Harriet Grove, which is broken off by her parents.

1810 Publishes the Gothic novel *Zastrozzi* in the spring and *Original Poetry by Victor and Cazire* in September. Enters University College, Oxford, in October and, with his student friend Thomas Jefferson Hogg, publishes *Posthumous Fragments of Margaret Nicholson* in November and his own novel *St Irvyne* in December.

1811 In January first meets his future wife Harriet Westbrook and in February, again with Hogg, publishes a pamphlet called *The Necessity of Atheism*, liberally distributing it among unsuitable university readers. Is sent down from Oxford in March when he refuses to answer questions about the pamphlet's authorship. Elopes with Harriet Westbrook, is married on 29 August in Edinburgh, and temporarily settles in the Lake District, where he meets a future polemical opponent, Robert Southey, sometime collaborator with Wordsworth and Coleridge.

1812 Campaigns in Dublin for Irish rehabilitation and emancipation. Publishes in this connection the pamphlets *An Address to, the Irish People*, *Proposals for an Association of Philanthropists*, and other broadsheets. On return to the mainland, he ends up in Tremadoc,

North Wales, writing his first major poem, *Queen Mab*, from September. Briefly joined by Elizabeth Hitchener, befriended through correspondence, who leaves in mutual recriminations in November when Shelley meets Thomas Love Peacock, poet and novelist to be, as well as one of his most friendly and astute critics; in London in December he meets William Godwin, famous as an anarchist philosopher, novelist, and man of letters generally, former husband of Mary Wollstonecraft, very influential in Shelley's thought as well as his future father-in-law.

1813 Convinced he is under threat in Tremadoc, he eventually returns to London, declaring his vegetarian tenets in *A Vindication of Natural Diet*, one of the notes to *Queen Mab*, itself published in May. Ianthe, the first of Shelley's two children by Harriet, born in June.

1814 *A Refutation of Deism* published. More meetings with Godwin and his daughter Mary, with whom he suddenly elopes in July, travelling to Switzerland, the party again a threesome with Mary's stepsister, Jane (subsequently Claire) Clairmont. The journey is eventually described in Percy's and Mary's *History of a Six Weeks' Tour*. Returns to London in September. Harriet gives birth to Shelley's and her son Charles in November.

1815 Mary's first child by Shelley is born in February and dies two weeks later. Grandfather Bysshe dies in January, initiating a settlement, resulting by June in an annual income for Shelley of £1,000 minus £200 to Harriet. Shelley's financial and personal affairs complicated further by loans to Godwin. Writes *Alastor* from August to September while living near and exploring the Thames at Windsor Great Park.

1816 Mary's second child, William, born in January. Publication of *Alastor . . . and Other Poems* in February. In May sets off for Switzerland, with family and Claire. There he makes friends with Lord Byron, who is engaging in an intermittent affair with Claire. Shelley begins 'Hymn to Intellectual Beauty', in late June, and, a month later, starts writing 'Mont Blanc'. Back in England in September, has to cope with suicides of

Mary's half-sister, Fanny Imlay, and of his wife Harriet. He marries Mary in December.

1817 Meets Keats, Leigh Hunt, and other 'Cockney' liberals. Claire gives birth to Allegra, her child by Byron, in January, and Shelley is not granted custody of his children by Harriet by Lord Eldon in March. By then he is in Marlow, writing *Laon and Cythna*, which he finishes in September, the same month as Clara Shelley is born. Keeps writing political pamphlets; *Laon and Cythna* is published and withdrawn in December, to be reissued as *The Revolt of Islam* in January 1818.

1818 Departs for Italy in March, never to return. Allegra sent to Byron, part of a series of arrangements which Shelley helps negotiate between Claire and Byron. In Leghorn (Livorno), then Bagni de Lucca, where he writes his essay 'On Love'. In Venice with Claire in August to discuss Allegra with Byron, eventually staying at Este. Clara Shelley, already unwell, dies, aged barely 1, after an arduous journey to Este then to Venice with Mary and William in September. Shelley begins 'Julian and Maddalo', writes Act I of *Prometheus Unbound*, and, increasingly estranged from Mary, travels to Rome and Naples.

1819 In Rome writes Acts II and III of *Prometheus Unbound* during March and April. William, aged 3, dies. Moves north to Leghorn, where he finishes *The Cenci* and 'The Mask of Anarchy' by September. In Florence he writes 'Ode to the West Wind' in October, *Peter Bell the Third*, the prose fragment 'On Life', and *A Philosophical View of Reform*. The survivor, Percy Florence Shelley, is born in November. Act IV of *Prometheus* finished by December, when he also writes the sonnet 'England in 1819'.

1820 The travels continue, now to Pisa in January, where 'The Sensitive-Plant' is composed, next back to Leghorn in June, where, amongst other poems, are written 'Ode to Liberty' and 'To A Skylark'. Once more in the Pisa area he produces 'The Witch of Atlas' the 'Ode to Naples', and meets Emilia Viviani in December.

1821 In January, Edward and Jane Williams come to Pisa. 'Epipsychidion' completed by February, when he begins *A Defence of Poetry*, finished in March. He begins

Adonais in May, publishing it in July. Writes *Hellas* in October. Byron moves to Pisa.

1822 Writing *Charles the First*. Arrival of Edward John Trelawney. In April, Claire's and Byron's daughter Allegra dies. The Shelleys and the Williams move to Lerici in April. Shelley begins *The Triumph of Life*. In June, Mary miscarries; Leigh Hunt and family arrive in Genoa and travel to Livorno. Shelley and Edward Williams drown in storm on return voyage to Lerici after visiting Hunt.

Abbreviations

Clark	*Shelley's Prose: Or, The Trumpet of a Prophecy*, ed. David L. Clark (Albuquerque, N.Mex.: University of New Mexico Press, 1966)
H&M	*Shelley: Poetical Works*, ed. Thomas Hutchinson, *A New Edition*, corrected by G. M. Matthews (London and New York: Oxford University Press, 1970)
Letters	*The Letters of Percy Bysshe Shelley*, ed. F. L. Jones (2 vols.; Oxford: Oxford University Press, 1964)
M&E	*The Poems of Shelley*, ed. Geoffrey Matthews and Kelvin Everest (3 vols. planned, one published so far: *1804–17*; London and New York: Longman, 1989–)
R&P	*Shelley's Poetry and Prose*, ed. Donald Reiman and Sharon B. Powers (New York and London: W. W. Norton and Co., 1977)
Rogers	*The Complete Poetical Works of Percy Bysshe Shelley*, ii. *1814–1817*, ed. Neville Rogers (Oxford: Oxford University Press, 1975)
Webb	*Percy Bysshe Shelley: Poems and Prose*, ed. Timothy Webb, critical selection by George E. Donaldson (London: J. M. Dent, 1995)

Abbreviations

1

Sources of the Self

The story of Shelley's youth is the story of his life, but not only because of his untimely death at the age of 29. His biographer immediately has to begin to defend or attack Shelley's intellectual and political seriousness. Early precociousness becomes indistinguishable from other characteristically impulsive identifications with interests radically different from those normally associated with his station in life. Hostile critics always find these gestures extravagant: Romantic in a pejorative or otherworldly sense, immature. For William Hazlitt, Shelley's speculative social solidarities were so implausible that they replaced one system of prejudice, the upper-class snobbery he should have had, with another.[1] For others, he was the essence of magnanimity, and, latterly, the type of that vanguard of revolution that sought the dissolution of its own privilege in the success of its emancipatory political mission. Precocious again, on principle. How did this exorbitant habit begin?

By all accounts Shelley enjoyed a happy childhood in the Sussex countryside as the son of a recently established landowning family living at Field Place, a fine house outside Horsham. Shelley's father, Timothy, inherited a baronetcy when grandfather Bysshe died in 1815. He became a Whig MP, capping a fairly adventurous family history with the dogged respectability of the shires. Shelley's mother, Elizabeth, although affectionate and intelligent, also reinforced the gentry stereotype. From this comfortable existence, fêted by sisters and retainers, Shelley was cast into the barbarity of the English public-school system, first at Syon House near Brentford, thereafter at Eton. He survived inventive bullying, eventually becoming liked for the singularity that had provoked his persecutions. At Eton, he was befriended by a Dr James Lind, who allowed him access to a library good enough to ground him in the many literary, scientific, and philosophical sources of his early poetry. He fell in love with his cousin, Harriet Grove, but the relationship broke up when the radicalism of his views on politics and religion became known to her parents. Their interferences, along with the resistant temperament developed in schoolboy conflicts, helped determine him in the anti-authoritarian attitudes for which he became famous. These took a definitive turn during the six months he next spent at University College, Oxford.

At Oxford, Shelley may have found time to study. He had already published *Zastrozzi*, his first Gothic novel, and *Original Poetry by Victor and Cazire* (H&M 843–57). Now followed *St Irvyne* and *Posthumous Fragments of Margaret Nicholson* (H&M 861–85). Nicholson had tried to assassinate George III, and proceeds from this collection went into a fund for the Irish journalist, Peter Finnerty, gaoled for criticizing the Government's military policy. Still more decisively for his Oxford career, Shelley collaborated with a friend, Thomas Jefferson Hogg, to produce anonymously a pamphlet called *The Necessity of Atheism*, which he sent to almost everyone in the University whom it might conceivably offend. The inevitable complaints led to the expulsion of the authors from Oxford. To this day there languishes in University College a marble effigy of Shelley rescued uncorrupted from the waves, a perfect image of his bowdlerized Victorian rehabilitation. This testimony to forgetfulness of the irritation he once caused the College is now a target only for student rowdies who feel threatened by the femininity of the pose.

The splendidly unequivocal title of the offending pamphlet spared most of the outraged the trouble of reading the contents. Yet, technically speaking, Shelley was not sent down from Oxford for holding obnoxious beliefs. As is obvious to the reader of *The Necessity of Atheism*, the pamphlet exculpates him from responsibility because it argues that all our beliefs are involuntary (Clark, 37–9). According to the pamphlet, Shelley's atheism could not be the creation of his own will. With the right evidence before us, the beliefs we consequently hold are beyond our power to disavow. To persecute people for their beliefs is thus totally pointless: they have no choice in the matter; they cannot change their minds. Conversely, no wishful thinking can substitute for lack of evidence and generate belief. Punishment for unbelief once more unfairly penalizes people for what they cannot remedy. University College's authorities wisely avoided an outright dispute with Shelley (or his brisk way with his sources in Spinoza and Hume) and dismissed him for, in effect, contempt of court: his principled refusal to answer their questions about the authorship of an anonymous pamphlet.

Shelley's first significant confrontation with authority thus turned on a question of authorship. However, his unwillingness personally to claim ownership of opinions that he thought to be true, and therefore to be the property of all, is also predictable from the argument of the pamphlet. His scepticism of authorship translates into a scepticism of authority. He attacks any person's or institution's pretension to know something other than truths that have arisen as naturally in them as they might have done in anyone else. This democratic view only undervalues the role of individual creativity, responsibility, and initiative in the eyes of those with a correspondingly diminished view of natural necessity: the chain of cause and effects explaining the inevitablity of what happens. Shelley's thought strives to content itself with its powers to sympathize with the material processes that produce it. In any case, the Master and Fellows of University College, in deciding to send Shelley down for the reasons they gave, were taking sides, whether they liked it or not, in the ancient philosophical dispute of freedom and necessity addressed by Shelley's pamphlet.

My emphasis in what follows is on Shelley's advocacy of a *creative* acceptance of natural necessity. Timely revisions of the Victorian portrayal of him as Matthew Arnold's 'ineffectual angel' often fall short of full recognition of this materialism, because they miss the point that for Shelley such openness to the forces that construct us is the ultimate creative effort.[2] This freedom to see beyond ourselves, and to identify with larger interests determining our own, is also an ultimately desirable sacrifice for Shelley because it simultaneously represents to him an image of his own radicalism. His modern interpreters have rightly put aside Shelley the fey escapist for a character seriously and definitively involved in politics. But Shelley's symptomatic imagining of revolutionary achievement as a kind of personal death links the true way in politics with his conclusions in metaphysics. The deep truth in both cases lacks an individual image because it rewrites individual as collective interests. Yet it is only in reaching this self-effacing conclusion that the individual can grasp his or her own essence: by reference, that is, to the community to which it naturally belongs. To see this desideratum as personal extinction betrays a class-nervousness about social reform. In *The Communist Manifesto*, Marx attacks the bourgeois for whom 'the disappearance of class culture is ... identical with the disappearance of all culture'.[3] But Shelley's anxiety also suggests the political charge residing in the otherwise highly abstract and purely philosophical problems of materialism. What happens to an idea of authority inseparable from the natural processes of mutability and decay to which all are subject? Analogously, can the poet convincingly embrace the democratic existence it has taken all his cultured privilege – all the resources of his distinctive philosophical and political wit – to imagine?

Shelley's writings put these questions in varied forms. His readers divide over their answers. For some, a glittering new mode of superstition replaces the old. Others, like Walter Bagehot, unsympathetic to Shelley's political views, nevertheless praise the exact and keen expressions of his self-surpassing – 'the acuteness of the mind seems to survive the mind itself'.[4] Shelley's own mode of self-understanding favours self-anatomizing, the exposure of the bodily features behind his ideas, over élitist mythopoeia. Even in those late conversation poems where he is most obviously talking to his sympathetic peers – appearing as Ariel, or the 'snake' (Byron's nickname for him), or wearing 'the idle mask of author' – coterie terminology is shot through with palpable bodily need: 'the secret food of fires unseen', 'hopes that can never die'. Here a physical longing for Jane Williams, the unobtainable wife of his close friend, Edward, explains his very private passion. Out of such erotic indigence Shelley makes a harmonious instrument, the guitar in 'With a Guitar to Jane' (R&P 449–51), which 'talks according to the wit/Of its companions' (ll. 82–3). With such reciprocity and gain in articulacy he hopes to civilize a passion that might otherwise become obsessive, on analogy with the way an artist has translated the guitar's material origins into expression and music 'To echo all harmonious thought' (l. 44).

Shelley's sense of being bodily determined was heightened by the variety of ailments from which he suffered throughout his life, and from the often frighteningly corrosive cures prescribed for them. He was struck by periodic spasms, all manner of nervous symptoms, and by ophthalmia. He was diagnosed as consumptive by one doctor he consulted; in retrospect, he appears more likely to have been experiencing nephritis, the agony of a descending kidney stone. Ill health was certainly one factor in his and his wife Mary's decision to live in Italy from 1818. Preoccupation with his body as a result of illness engaged him imaginatively as well. He was to some extent a hypochondriac; he may even, as has recently been claimed, have thought himself syphilitic.[5] Syphilis, fully described, seems capable of accounting for almost all forms of physical devastation; Shelley's infection, therefore, remains a possibility. The range of syphilitic symptoms also helps explain its metaphorical existence in most of his figurations of that estrangement from the bodily his poetry resisted, that morbid corporeality always threatening to engulf his contrasting sympathies and attunement to myriad material associations with the universe around him.

The rights of the body, properly acknowledged, overcame the artificial distance between mind and matter maintained by the establishment ideologues Shelley opposed. They left the democratic body to rot and erected superstitious hierarchies favourable to Church and State and King. Politically, the return of the repressed body is perfectly imaged at the moment in Shelley's late, incomplete drama, *Charles the First* (H&M 488–507) when a second citizen (republican soubriquet) describes the neglected rabble of Caroline imperium as 'At once the sign and the thing signified' (I. 168). In context, the integrity of sign and signified opposes the ideological separation maintained by a court culture keen to derive its legitimacy from sources higher than its economic subordination of the body politic. Excluded from privilege, but nevertheless necessary to its possibility, Shelley's 'troop of cripples, beggars, and lean outcasts' are here inextricably part of the meaning of what is 'signified' by a better class of people than they.

> Here is health
> Followed by grim disease, glory by shame,
> Waste by lame famine, wealth by squalid want.
>
> (I. 162–4)

Each group's meaning, semiotically and politically, is founded on its difference from the other. A 'Youth' quickly tries to counter the second citizen's implication by placing the dispossessed as 'The anti-masque [that] serves as discords do in sweetest music'. But his aestheticism gives art the ideological function of representing as natural an arbitrary ascendancy of one section of society over another. Difference is only difference. In his essay 'On Life' of 1819 Shelley wrote that 'almost all familiar objects are signs, standing not for themselves but for others'. Not to see and pursue the ideological connections of things, the meaning in their difference, is to remain in the 'error' in which 'our whole life is thus an education' (R&P 477).

Shelley's bodily troubles, so prominent a feature of his life and letters, do not only represent personal difficulties to be overcome. They show the temptation generally to regard escape from the material conditions of life as our ultimate vocation. Shelley identified this mistaken view with an ideological use of religion to repress political reform. Another temptation is to gloss as bodily and fixed what can in fact be reformed by being realigned semiotically, placed in different relations to the other things that give that thing meaning. His own imaginative activity aimed to redirect escape from individual hardship and limitation away from an other-worldly destination and back to material conditions understood more generously as the source of all sorts of new personal, social, and physical relations.

Shelley most concisely confronts the limits of these constructive identifications, or what his friend the radical journalist and Cockney poet Leigh Hunt called 'an exceeding sympathy with the whole universe, material and intellectual',[6] in the famous sonnet he wrote at the end of 1817, 'Ozymandias'.

> I met a traveller from an antique land,
> Who said – 'Two vast and trunkless legs of stone
> Stand in the desert... near them, on the sand
> Half-sunk, a shattered visage lies, whose frown,
> And wrinkled lip, and sneer of cold command,
> Tell that its sculptor well those passions read
> Which yet survive, stamped on these lifeless things,
> The hand that mocked them, and the heart that fed;
> And on the pedestal these words appear:

"My name is Ozymandias, King of Kings,
Look on my works ye Mighty, and despair!"
Nothing beside remains. Round the decay
Of that colossal Wreck, boundless and bare,
The lone and level sands stretch far away'. –[7]

For *both* the tyrant, Ozymandias, and his sculptor critic, the 'lone and level sands' presage the same dissolution. The sculptor's critical advantage is maintained for a while. Ruination of the statue makes Ozymandias' pretensions ridiculous but only enhances the sculpture's expressivity, at least within a Romantic taste for sublimely suggestive fragments. But eventually even that ironic commentary on the tyrant will succumb to the same erosion. Against this pessimistic interpretation, one could argue that, while the power of Ozymandias crumbles, the story told by the sculptor can be passed on, its truth intact, through a succession of relays – 'the traveller from an antique land' who deciphers the sculpture, the narrator whom he tells of his experience, endless readers of the poem. To become one's readers is a kind of figurative immortality that Shelley tries hard to find satisfying. Ozymandias' monumental boast is either self-refuting or a caveat to the rest of the 'Mighty'. The poet's satire, though, can be reinterpreted to apply to different historical circumstances, other tyrannies, even to the Hanoverian monarchy of Shelley's own day. After all, he wrote the sonnet in friendly competition with his parodist friend, Horace Smith, whose own offering analogously imagined 'Where London stood . . . some fragment huge' (Webb, app. 3, 463). 'Poetry', as Shelley bravely claimed in *A Defence of Poetry* (R&P 478–508) a few years later, 'is a sword of lightning, ever unsheathed, which consumes the scabbard that would contain it . . . Poetry, and the principle of Self . . . are the God and the Mammon of the world' (R&P 491, 503).

Yet, stepping out of the framework of Romantic enthusiasm, we must ask the question of how far it can make sense so to sacrifice a principle of self to the lastingness of poetry. How consoling is purely metaphorical immortality? As the 'Ode to the West Wind' (R&P 221–3) puts the problem, even when the dissemination of personal influence persuades us with the authority of an elemental force, can we, should we, ever forget the pathos of the individual sacrifice involved? Equally, we can query how far a poem's significance can change over time and still retain an integrity that faithfully prolongs its original meaning.[8] Shelley's *A Defence* aligns poetry squarely with modernity. It was written in 1821 as a response to his friend Thomas Love Peacock's *The Four Ages of Poetry,* which attacked poetry as an outmoded, reactionary discourse. Shelley, taking 'a more general view of what is Poetry' than Peacock (*Letters,* ii. 275), emphasizes a 'vitally metaphorical' use of language fundamental to the task of keeping knowledge relevant and up to date (R&P 482). If we cannot apply moral, political, historical, scientific, and economic wisdom, transforming their meanings to suit different contexts, these knowledges are useless. Furthermore, if we cannot see beyond current uses to new applications, our knowledge will have no future, will rot in the sand. Both these kinds of applications show a metaphorical imagination at work, enlarging our susceptibility to previously 'unapprehended combinations of thought'.

This power of transference, or 'higher criticism' as it was then called, can appear to be sufficient explanation of Shelley's poetics. But part of the meaning of *A Defence* is to be fraught, like all his writings, with the anxieties we have been cataloguing. Shelley's implication of poetry in the production of modernity, even postmodernity, is problematic, although in proportion as it genuinely anticipates uncertainties typical of our own time. Andrew Bennett has written astutely of Shelley's paradoxical success.[9] In reassuringly allying itself to technological progress, translation, and transformation into new media, poetry has to submit to new imponderables. Confidence of one's immortality in print, or of the survival of one's writings for juster appreciation by audiences of the future, goes with the worrying realization that one does not know who one is writing for. And, if the latter is true, we cannot predict the meanings that posterity will read into our work. In *Prometheus Unbound* (R&P 130–210), for example, Jesus' words 'outlived him' and in Christianity became the 'swift poison' he is heard lamenting (I. 548–55). 'The seeking [through fame] of a sympathy with the unborn and unknown', Shelley had written despondently to his friends, the Gisbornes, less than a year before beginning his heroic *Defence,* 'is a feeble mode of allaying the love within us' (*Letters,* ii. 206–7). A technological afterlife still extinguishes subjectivity: no longer in control of the significance of what you have written, you can no longer regard your work as the lasting expression of personality. But it was just some sense of a personal importance living on beyond one's temporality that a print culture had seemed to guarantee. There appear to be only two ways out of this dilemma, and Shelley tries to take both of them.

The first is to believe that in fact you do know what future audiences are going to be like and so can foretell their predispositions as readers. Shelley's persistent necessitarianism does commit him to believing in the progressive amelioration and enlightenment of human society. In writing for a better people than exists now, Shelley's poet anticipates what will happen by prophetically summoning that future audience. Currently 'unacknowledged', poetry is nevertheless the idiom in which we can legislate for the truth to come. The second way out of postmodern indeterminacy is to accept it: to possess a sense of identity unthreatened by the prospect of its dissemination among future audiences. Self-expression then survives as part of the collective productivity of meaning typical of the humanity to which it belongs. Originating as the unique utterance of a privileged individual, poetry is confirmed as such by becoming the facilitating idiom of everyone. However sanguine Shelley tries to be about these two solutions in the theory of *A Defence*, his poetry written immediately after it confirms his scepticism of the first (*Hellas* (R&P 406–40)) and his fear of the second (*Adonais* (R&P 388–406)); these twin responses run through his poetry and reach their culminating paroxysm in *The Triumph of Life* (R&P 453–70). Shelley's work ends with a pessimism that has to be its own reward. *The Triumph* evinces a discontent with our lot so basic as to persuade us that our true grounding lies elsewhere, and must be better than this. Since we can hardly be conscious of an alternative to 'Life' – hence our necessary pessimism – we should none the less greet with a lightening of the spirit those self-transforming processes whose revolutionary character might otherwise appear unequivocally destructive.

2

The Politics of Imagined Communities

Although pessimism has little place in Shelley's early enthusiasm, the philosophical framework that was to produce it is sliding into place. Shelley's presumption in setting off at the age of 19 to Dublin in order to address the Irish people on how to resist their persecution sounds unattractively precocious. The audience he envisaged for his pamphlet *An Address to the Irish People* (Clark, 39–60) was the 'poor Catholics'; from the start, the invitation to talk down to or patronize them looks irresistible. However, Shelley's youthful polemic becomes a more sophisticated exercise, one already expressive of his problematic idealism. He appears to have written the pamphlet prior to any empirical research into the true condition of the Irish. His 'Postscript' damagingly concedes that only now, after writing it, has he 'endeavoured to make [himself] more accurately acquainted with the state of the public mind on those great topics of grievances which induced [him] to select Ireland as a theatre, the widest and fairest, for the operations of the determined friend of religious and political freedom' (Clark, 59). Did he only bother travelling to Dublin to tell the Irish of their usefulness in offering his radical opinions more dramatic support? This appearance of unpleasant opportunism is modified by Shelley's actual argument. His idealistic adoption of the Irish to bear 'the standard of liberty...a flag of fire – a beacon at which the world shall light the torch of Freedom!' is bound up with his attack on their religious sectarianism and propensity to violent rebellion (Clark, 43). The details of their plight are precisely what he wants them to transcend in the interests of generally desirable political principles. His cavalier attitude towards their circumstances is to encourage them to enlarge their aspirations beyond confrontational struggle between fixed identities and nationalities. Far from being condescending, Shelley urges on them that escape from restricting oppositions to be exemplified by his most exalted poetic heroes and heroines.

Shelley's abstraction, then, has a practical purpose. His pragmatism is evident first in his silencing of his own atheism to sue instead for Catholic Emancipation. Secondly, he muffles his hatred of aristocracy to lament, like Maria Edgeworth and others, the passing of a *responsible* Irish aristocracy with the Act of Union of 1802. He also believed his intervention was called for because the new Prince Regent looked unlikely to continue in the enthusiasm for Catholic Emancipation once instilled in him by Charles James Fox. How might Shelley's characteristic pacifism be comparably strategic?

Shelley commends a pacifism that demands moral and intellectual rather than physical resistance, opposition that conspicuously occupies a moral high ground aspired to by all and so shames its opponents into becoming its supporters. When the youthful Shelley urges the Irish to '*Reform Yourselves*', he appears priggish, even racist, in his presumption. But, as a political tactic, Shelley's advice puts into practice a Godwinian scepticism of the ultimate utility of Government. Moral rehabilitation prior to institutional reform cannot be called rebellious or revolutionary. But in seeming to be the opposite of interference in the apparatus of the State, it nevertheless initiates an extra-parliamentary opposition and takes a step along the Godwinian road towards an imagined polity 'when no government will be wanted but that of your neighbour's opinion' (Clark, 51). Such confidence in consensus assumes shared principles arrived at through discussion. In *Proposals for an Association of Philanthropists* (Clark, 60–70), a redaction for a more educated audience of the ideas of *An Address*, Shelley offers as a reassuringly 'safe method of improvement' the institution of a philanthropic 'association' whose activities are far from the secret meetings, mob violence, and openly rebellious radicalism condemned in *An Address*. His 'association' is to be 'obnoxious to the government, though nothing would be further from the views of associated philanthropists than attempting to subvert establishments forcibly, or even hastily' (Clark, 62–3). Carefully read, this disclaimer does not appear to rule out all subversion from the philanthropic purpose of association, just violent or revolutionary subversion. The apparent moderation disguises a more extreme radicalism that wants, anarchistically, to do away with government altogether. The influence of Shelley's future father-in-law is now obvious.

Poetry, though, plays an even more important role in articulating Shelley's radicalism. Civil society, on the model sketched in *An Address* and *Proposals*, should cohere simply because of people's ability to communicate with each other. 'Think, read, and talk' is Shelley's repeated advice to the politically aspirant Irish (Clark, 49). Poetry is nothing if not a self-conscious excellence in that power to communicate, and one similarly ideal in its endeavours and targets. Its legislation, as *A Defence* will argue, is unrecognized by the positive institutions actually ordering our social behaviour. The associations for the communication of philanthropy that Shelley wants to encourage are comparably innocent of political content. But Shelley's arguments are equally disingenuous in either case. Mere communication is politically unaccountable because of the comprehensiveness not the modesty of the alternatives that associations for that purpose might offer to existing political structures.

To some extent this threat had been appreciated by the authorities in the 1790s when Paine's immensely popular *The Rights of Man* was burned by the mob and members of corresponding societies put on trial as much for their structural threat as extra-parliamentary groupings as for the moderate reforms they might recommend. Edmund Burke starts his polemical *Reflections on the Revolution in France* with just such an attack on Dissenting culture for its claims to unelected representativeness of British opinion. Almost twenty years later, Shelley's Irish servant Daniel Healy (or Hill) spent six months in prison after fly-posting Shelley's *A Declaration of Rights* (Clark, 70–2), a numbered digest of the main points of *An Address*. But the need to re-imagine the social contract in open discussion again became pressing, especially after victory in war, so often a catalyst for progressive political change in Britain. Shelley's radicalism partook of the general shift of opinion leading to the first Reform

Act of 1832. The persistent parallels between his political and his poetic idealism, however, show the far greater lengths to which his reforming zeal aspired long after he had given up doctrinaire allegiance to Godwin's anarchism. It is just as true to say that only if we preserve this parallel can we keep in focus the profoundly *political* activity Shelley took poetry to be. Poetry is legislation for him; and it remains unacknowledged because it expresses too generous an understanding of what human beings have in common – emotionally, sexually, ethically, culturally – for the politicians to handle.

Shelley tells us in his 'Essay on Christianity' (Clark, 196–215) that the 'only perfect and genuine republic is that which comprehends every living being' (Clark, 208). Is he being frivolously idealistic? Should we immediately correct him with other quotations from his own *A Proposal for Putting Reform to the Vote* (1817) (Clark, 158–62), which regards universal suffrage as perilous and advocates retention of a tax-paying qualification? But 'a pure republic', even in *A Proposal*, remains 'the fittest to produce the happiness and promote the genuine eminence of man' (Clark, 162). In fact this ideal political vision can be recast in quite a tough, recognizably modern idiom.

Shelley argues perpetually that the quality of politics is largely dependent on an effort of imagination. The more the relations between people are sympathetically taken into account, the more humanely can they be accommodated politically. This might sound like a totalitarian piety, rolling forward the power of the state to legislate for all aspects of life, however private and individualistic. An opposite deregulation, on the other hand, cannot distinguish between cases when it genuinely honours and when it curtails freedom. 'The great secret of morals is Love', wrote Shelley provocatively in *A Defence of Poetry* (R&P, 487). But his idealism translates into the realistic view that the enlightened self-interest extolled by Adam Smith, and so influential in the explanations of political economy dominant in Shelley's day, stands in need of supplementation. Society works as much through a different interest in social justice and diversity, in the different ways in which people can be happy and fulfilled. In other words, it is unlikely that the social climate will improve if people see that it is not changing out of consideration for their hardships but only in order to reproduce a more efficient workforce. The latter, Shelley's phrase suggests, can be achieved only as a rewarding side effect of the former. In quite a hard-headed sense, therefore, Shelley claims it necessary to prioritize this sensitivity to welfare over its symbiotic economic value through a continually sustained imaginative effort. Of a society that thinks in this idiom, Shelley can say as he did of republican Rome in *A Defence of Poetry* that its 'true poetry...lived in its institutions', and that its great statesmen 'were at once the poets and actors' of contemporary political dramas. Shelley highlights the unlikely quality of the political material he is here compelled to make sense of poetically. 'These things are not the less poetry, quia carent *vate sacro* (because they lack an inspired bard)' (R&P 494). Only by the poetic means of mutual sympathy can a coherent and patriotic state be perfected. Only as a result of such imaginative facility will the polity hang together and secular well-being be realized.

Shelley typically claims both that we need to use imagination, a poetic faculty, to unveil reality, and that it is reality that excites rather than constrains imaginative power. In this credo he speaks the dialect of Romantic irony, but his political inflection of it especially recalls Rousseau. According to Rousseau's *Émile, ou l'éducation*, human development results from a progressive appreciation of human limitation. But the whole force of human institutions is to carry us vainly and artificially beyond these normal boundaries, and it takes real civic imagination to restore them to natural proportions. We must learn to recognize necessity; all other subordination or aspiration is frivolous. Could we but observe the general will, 'dependence on men would become dependence on things again', common interests that we constitutionally share and against which no selfishness can triumph. This rephrases Shelleyan philanthropy, but behind Rousseau lie sources in another Romantic hero, Spinoza, and his tenet that 'in so far as we understand, we can desire nothing save that which is necessary', becoming detached from purely individual interests in the process.[1] Perhaps the Roman poet Lucretius is ultimately responsible for envisaging this social community formed through the apprehension of a common natural dispensation. In teaching us of the nature of things, Lucretius strives to set us free from the tough knots of superstition, religious and political.

My previous sentence freely translates the epigraph from *De rerum natura* standing at the head of Shelley's first major poem, *Queen Mab* (M&E 265–424), along with other tags from the Enlightenment *philosophe* Voltaire and the Greek philosopher and physicist Archimedes. Shelley was trying to get hold of Spinoza's works in 1812, and Rousseau is a haunting and ambiguous presence throughout all his writings. Shelley's early purchase on this materialist tradition helps situate and explain further his development of typically Romantic concepts of sympathy and imagination. Imaginative sympathy need not, as is often thought, license a sentimental escape from scientific rigour. Shelley's materialism drives his version of the eighteenth-century debate in English thought concerning the connection between sympathy and an objective sense of justice. Thinkers from Shaftesbury to Hume and Smith argue that just estimations of actions depend on the ability to abstract oneself from personal circumstances and occupy the position of an impartial spectator. From this point of view we are sympathetically responsive to common standards of behaviour we would demand of ourselves were we in others' shoes. The paradox of making impartiality the goal of sympathy parallels Shelley's understanding of material reality as the goal of imagination – that ironic *discovery* of necessity both painful to the creative self then required to submit to it and liberating in its levelling of the false moral and authoritarian pretensions of others. From *The Necessity of Atheism* onwards, Shelley claimed with Spinoza that belief was involuntary. Were we to be shown the truth, we would necessarily accept it. But acceptance of what Rousseau called 'the heavy yoke of necessity' is difficult to achieve, and requires an imaginative breach of inherited repressions and ideologies – a pessimistic, poetic discontent with received world-pictures.[2] This is the struggle that Shelley's poems successively unfold.

Shelley's commentators frequently sense a conflict between his poetic and scientific motives. He himself expressed his scepticism of reconciling them most unequivocally in a letter to Peacock of 1819: 'I consider Poetry very subordinate to moral & political science, & if I were well, certainly I should aspire to the latter' (*Letters*, ii. 71). The remark pinpoints a moment of estrangement in a lifelong drama of reconciliation. Peacock, after all, was the addressee of *A Defence*. Both poetic and scientific interests had to surrender cherished privileges. The individual poet is repeatedly figured by Shelley as a casualty of his taxing vision of our common nature, political and biological.[3] From *Alastor* (R&P 69–87) to *Adonais*, Shelley's narrators threaten to disintegrate under the pressure to exercise unrestrained poetic sympathy. This is not to say that Shelley must subscribe to his narrator's visions. The poems are often better read as registering but criticizing an inherited Romantic poetic discourse that offers no escape from understanding our necessary absorption by larger forces as personal extinction. Matching the instability of this poetic self-critique are scientific ambitions compromised by Shelley's ineluctably poetic idiom. In a letter of 1812, Shelley could have been describing the decade of his remaining life when he wrote of reading 'whatever metaphysics came in my way, without however renouncing poetry, an attachment to which has characterised all my wanderings and changes' (*Letters*, i. 303). His later work, though, showed that for him a full scientific admission of the power of natural necessity required a poetry productively at odds with itself, whether figured in the 'silence, solitude and vacancy' of 'Mont Blanc', the 'imageless' deep truth of *Prometheus Unbound*, or the vision-erasing *Triumph of Life*.

3

Against the Self-Images of the Age

The nine cantos of *Queen Mab* (M&E 265–424) open in unlikely fashion for a poem that was to become, as G. B. Shaw was later told by one of them, 'the Chartists' Bible'. Its intent, though, is to revive a discourse uniting scientific and political scepticism, one associated with the materialism of Locke and the *philosophes* and traditionally thought inimical to the Romantic imagination. The opening of Shelley's major début dispels all that:

> How wonderful is Death,
> Death and his brother Sleep!
> One, pale as yonder waning moon
> With lips of lurid blue;
> The other, rosy as the morn
> When throned on ocean's wave
> It blushes o'er the world:
> Yet both so passing wonderful!
>
> (I. 1–8)

From the start the poem challenges us to find alluring the dissemination of individual self-consciousness. Initial echoes of the earliest Greek literature, Hesiod's mythology and Homer's epithets, mingle with those of early English Romanticism. Shelley pointedly resituates and develops the opening of *Thalaba the Destroyer* (1801), a revolutionary romance penned by the sometime radical Robert Southey, now turned Tory, whom Shelley had met and argued with at length in December 1811, the year before he wrote *Queen Mab*. Shelley's allusive recovery of literary and political innocence prepares for the image of a sleeping girl, Ianthe, who arrests the chariot of the fairy queen, Mab, in her celestial flight. Photic and kinetic fantasy then unite in this figure of Queen Mab, who rewards the virtuous Ianthe by transporting her soul ('The perfect semblance of its bodily frame') to the vantage point of her palace. Its eminence affords astronomical and chronological insights, improving this time on Volney's panoramic *Les Ruines, ou méditations sur les révolutions des empires* (1791), which had fuelled the scepticism of the last generation of radicals. Ianthe is told the laws of universal history and the history of the universe; each is as observant of the other's causal patterns as Ianthe's soul is reproductive of her body's shape. The heady mixture of different visionary idioms elaborates the poem's materialism, its version of an animism common to French and English radical thinkers from *philosophes* like Holbach to Dissenting theorists like Erasmus Darwin:

> There's not one atom of yon earth
> But once was living man;
> Nor the minutest drop of rain,
> That hangeth in its thinnest cloud,
> But flowed in human veins...
>
> (II. 211–15)

Again, these lines implicate natural and human history. Just as no material particle of earth exists that might not have once been human fabric, so every spot on earth, however barren now, has its historical tale to tell. 'Thou canst not find one spot/Whereon no city stood' (II. 223–4). This exaggerates Enlightenment historicizations of nature, and perhaps explicitly draws on the catastrophic theories of Cuvier, Buffon, and others, to be used in Byron's *Cain* (1821), which attack the present's idea of its own uniqueness or modernity, relativizing it physically and culturally. According to much Enlightenment historiography, we may only be repeating a previous catastrophe. The suggestion that others were always there before us puts in perspective claims, usually religious, that typically require us to be unique, enjoying a vocation radically separate from that recorded for everything else in natural history. Similarly undermined is any establishment's boast to be all-powerful, free of the cycle of history that has levelled all authoritarian pretensions in the past. Increasingly, as we have seen, Shelley addresses the personal cost of his radical scepticism. In the first flush of youthful confidence, though, only 'the vain-glorious mighty of the earth' seem agonized by the mutability eroding their dreams of eternity. In *Queen Mab* monarch and subject 'for ever play/A losing game into each other's hands' (III. 172–3) simply because tyranny is mutually demeaning. Shelley still has to get in focus the self-defeating character of authority itself. That deeper scepticism requires him to reconceive authority: to locate it in impersonal processes beyond individual control, while simultaneously expressing the pain and despair caused him by such a concession.

The infusion of Shelley's radicalism with this tragic and personal note – the calculated bathos of his personal appearances in 'Ode to the West Wind' and *Adonais*, for example – suggests consciousness of the fragility of his own cultural and class privileges within the transformed society to which his radicalism leads him. In *Queen Mab*, political apotheosis can be seen only from a literally extraterrestial viewpoint; in later poems, the narrative is situated within specific societies, and the poetic vision counts the cost of losing the benefits that have helped to produce it. A much more complex poetry results, one whose reforming vision is not just modified but deepened by what Donald Davie once picked out as Shelley's distinctive 'urbanity'.[1] An urbane style allows the narrator to reflect upon causes and effects with a disinterestedness persuasive because he is too sophisticated to exclude himself from his review. Like visionary materialism, tragic urbanity is a helpful oxymoron in the attempt critically to get on terms with Shelley's style.

Just as his political theory tried to see a political end beyond the need for government, so Shelley's poetry looks beyond its own conventional demarcations to sacrifice the authority of the poet to the greater good of literary history. While this is the great theme of *A Defence of Poetry*, it is also the fundamental pathos of the predominantly lyrical, self-expressive mode in which Shelley's poetry articulates such self-denial. In *Queen Mab*, though, Shelley's poetry does not yet possess the self-critical flexibility that his political prose (and the copious prose notes he wrote for the poem) hint it will have to acquire. Poetry has still to become the richly communicative instrument standing in for corrupt ideas of political society. In *Queen Mab*, it confidently ventriloquizes the magniloquent spirit of Nature and denounces contrasting 'mockeries of earthly power' – ideologies, usually religious, by which tyrants falsely imitate ('mock') natural inevitability (IV. 220). Mab's long tirade then anathematizes the 'Twin-sister of religion, selfishness!', love prostituted commercially – 'All things are sold' – and the 'unenjoying sensualism' of pleasures taken without regard to relationship (V. 22, 177, 195). Poetry typically imagines another kind of commerce, the 'commerce of sincerest virtue', the 'commerce of good words and works', its sympathies translating immediately into a social programme (V. 231, 253). Poetry does not proudly despise literal, economic idioms, but works unselfishly in their service to imagine authentic meanings for them. Otherwise, as *A Defence* puts it, we lack 'the creative faculty to imagine that which we know... we want the poetry of life' (R&P, 502).

At the end of *Queen Mab*, Ianthe's spirit is reunited with her body and she awakens to Henry and his 'speechless love' (IX. 238). It is unclear how the 'lore' she has 'learned' (IX. 141) from Mab is compatible with this domestic resting place. As I have been arguing, Shelley's mature poetry starts from that question. But the immense popularity of *Queen Mab* amongst later working-class radicals must in part have derived from his uncompromising refocusing of a high-art form upon those issues that such discourse had traditionally excluded. The notes, expanding on Shelley's recent pamphlets, more obviously account for *Queen Mab*'s popularity in progressive circles. But they also raise the issue of what value is added to them by the poetic expression they prosaically annotate. Exceptionally, Milton had written visionary poetry in a language partly continuous with the religious political dialect of radical sectaries of the 1640s and 1650s. Shelley similarly tries to throw a bridge across the gap between high and low, and periodically renews these negotiations in later poems. 'O happy Earth! reality of Heaven!' (IX. 1) is the reiterated conclusion of Mab's imaginative realism: the farthest reach of imagination is to perceive its own earthly origins. In the preceding canto, Mab envisages a golden future when 'man has lost/His terrible prerogative, and stands/An equal amidst equals' (VIII. 225–7). While dismaying Shelley's theistical opponents, the conclusions of *Queen Mab* require another faith: that this new, egalitarian dispensation will not extinguish the distinctive imagination that conceived it. Yet Shelley has to accept that, in this ideal homecoming, social disparities will vanish, and imagining and knowing will no longer contradict each other. Not to believe this is to occupy the position of Ahasuerus in the poem, a constitutionally homeless character, the symbiotic opposite of the Christian establishment: 'a wondrous phantom, from the dreams / Of human error's dense and purblind faith' (VII. 64–5). Hence, Ahasuerus is the wandering Jew, the fantasized other of Christian prejudice, 'this phantasmal portraiture / Of wandering human thought' (VII. 274–5).

Queen Mab shows the imaginative bravura needed if, in despite of vested interests, including its own, we are to invoke 'Necessity! thou mother of the world!' (VI. 198). Shelley here quotes Holbach, as editors point out, and without sentimentalizing matter and endowing the constituents of the universe with feeling and purpose, he proclaims the imaginative sympathy with matter needed to countenance the evolution out of it of our affective nature. We must not, Mab's vision claims, understand this truth as a reduction or trivialization of the human, but as its articulation through a nature larger than our individuality:

I tell thee that those viewless beings,
Whose mansion is the smallest particle
Of the impassive atmosphere,
Think, feel and live like man;
That their affections and antipathies,
Like his, produce the laws
Ruling their moral state;
And the minutest throb
That through their frame diffuses
The slightest, faintest motion,
Is fixed and indispensable
As the majestic laws
That rule yon rolling orbs.

(II. 231–43)

Queen Mab sets the pattern for Shelley's subsequent intertwining of human with natural history and for his endowment of nature with the self-reflexivity of mind.[2] Neither habit indicates a pathetic fallacy but catches Shelley's Romantic fascination with the production of consciousness out of natural elements. The quest for this formative moment is the story told by *Alastor, or the Spirit of Solitude* (R&P 69–87).

Alastor was published in February 1816. It appeared in the company of eleven other poems, most recalling Shelley's immediate predecessors, Wordsworth and Coleridge, and criticizing their achievement. In Shelley's sonnet 'To Wordsworth' (M&E 454–5), Wordsworth is a deserter of 'Songs consecrate to truth and liberty' (l. 12). According to 'O! There are Spirits of the Air' (M&E 447–50), Coleridge has arrived at a settled stasis induced by his pursuit of ideals perversely substituting for social or personal relationships. *Alastor,* Shelley's most ambitious poem of the collection, continues the critique. Wordsworth's decline from this admirable self-sufficiency, lamented by the sonnet, has become the dilemma *Alastor* dramatizes. Wordsworth was 'as a lone star, whose light did shine / On some frail bark in winter's midnight roar' (ll. 7–8), the guiding light of adventurers such as the visionary so precariously afloat in his 'shallop' in *Alastor*. The Preface's quotation from Wordsworth's 1814 *Excursion*, 'The good die first...', targets a defeatism redeemed only in religious conviction or the transcendence gained through solitary self-exploration. The poem's exoticism also engages with the unabashedly imperialist purpose trumpeted in *The Excursion*'s final book. The rehabilitation experienced by the main characters in colloquy amid Lakeland isolation during Wordsworth's long poem is meant to inspire, even command, the proselytizing of its benefits to other lands. By contrast, Shelley's orientalism in *Alastor* is riven with self-doubt and contradiction. Its epigraph, from Augustine's *Confessions,* suggests the paradox of trying in introspective solitude to seize poetically on self-confirming emotions like love, which, by definition, should only arise in response to others. The exoticizing of the Eastern target of British imperialism by *Alastor*'s narrator and poet-hero comparably effaces the formative role of other people in shaping our identity.[3]

Encouragement not to identify with the poet-hero comes principally from the Preface.

> The poem entitled 'ALASTOR' may be considered as allegorical of one of the most interesting situations of the human mind. It represents a youth of uncorrupted feelings and adventurous genius led forth by an imagination inflamed and purified through familiarity with all that is excellent and majestic, to the contemplation of the universe. He drinks deep of the fountains of knowledge, and is still insatiate.

> The magnificence and beauty of the external world sinks profoundly into the frame of his conceptions, and affords to their modifications a variety not to be exhausted. So long as it is possible for his desires to point towards objects thus infinite and unmeasured, he is joyous, and tranquil, and self-possessed. But the period arrives when these objects cease to suffice. His mind is at length suddenly awakened and thirsts for intercourse with an intelligence similar to itself. He images to himself the Being whom he loves... He seeks in vain for a prototype of his conception. Blasted by his disappointment, he descends to an untimely grave. (M&E 462–3)

Scepticism of the poem's narrator is then invited by the Wordsworthian language in which he frequently idealizes the poet's fate, finally summoning from Wordsworth's 'Ode: Intimations of Immortality' 'a woe "too deep for tears" (l. 713). Much as the poet did, his narrator appears to generate a love-object rather than to respond to it. Nevertheless, as the second paragraph of this tricky introduction to the poem tells us, this is a 'generous error' . Those who do not commit it are 'meaner spirits' who yet 'keep aloof from sympathies with their kind' and are 'morally dead' (M&E 463).

In *Alastor*, then, the 'self-centred seclusion' of the poet leads him to fall in love with his own imaginings instead of another person. This fault nevertheless produces the poetry we are to enjoy as readers. A potential lover for the poet is at hand in the representative figure of the enamoured 'Arabian maid'. In ignoring her, he incurs the wrath of 'the spirit of sweet human love'. But his fantasies are nevertheless of as high an order as those reprehensibly deserted by the younger Wordsworth: the poet's dream-woman fascinates because

> Knowledge and truth and virtue were her theme,
> And lofty hopes of divine liberty,
> Thoughts the most dear to him, and poesy,
> Herself a poet.
>
> (ll.. 158–61)

At this point the poem could be asserting that true poetic ideals demand physical realization; hence the poet understandably tries to make love to the phantom embodying them. When he wakes to find her gone, he suffers from a postponement of his ideal, a frustration that it is the traditional purpose of a certain kind of art, along with religion, to make tolerable. Conversely, we might feel invited to read the passage when he, 'yielding to the irresistible joy,/With frantic gesture and short breathless cry/ Folded his frame in her dissolving arms' (ll. 185–7) as telling us of the self-defeatingness of imaginatively simulated relationships. Overall, though, the poem dramatizes the need to negotiate these two positions. Although acknowledging that our sense of identity is not self-originating, the poem concedes that it is imaginatively created in the responses of those we feel sympathetic to us.

This gloss partly comes from Shelley's essay 'On Love' (R&P 473–4), written almost three years later. There, our 'likeness' is not a psychological datum but something we desire: the 'ideal prototype' encapsulating our authentic potential can itself be estimated only by the imagination of another, our 'antitype', our perfect lover. In the unsurprising absence of sufficiently sympathetic individuals, we seek this identity-conferring association through comunication with nature, an environment transformed into our native respondent as if by 'the enthusiasm of patriotic success'. We are clearly on the brink of substituting imaginary for interpersonal relationships here, but the man not so tempted 'becomes the living sepulchre of himself' – another of the 'morally dead'. 'On Love' uses ideal categories to avoid prejudging personal development and growth. A perpetually unfolding identity is elaborated through its power of association, not just epistemologically but socially, sexually, ethically, and environmentally. These imagined reciprocities are a self-developing mechanism very different from introspection. They explain how the self's identity progressively evolves in practice, a process quite distinct from original creativity, 'Primary Imagination', or 'the One life' sought out in the poetry of Coleridge and Wordsworth. That specular quest, quintessentially Romantic, is the narcissistic error charted by *Alastor*'s poet-hero's journey.

For the poet of *Alastor*, and the narrator who puts words into his mouth, ultimate significance is a consciousness of one's own creativity. Meaning 'flashed like strong inspiration' as he pursued an originary knowledge – 'The thrilling secrets of the birth of time' (ll. 126–8). Increasingly, he seems to be in quest of personal extinction rather than dissemination. According to the poem's mentor, Augustine, 'there is no time before the world began'.[4] Shelley's other writings also imply that consciousness of ourselves and of history is produced by the diversification of experience in time; it is not contained in perfect embryo, the better deciphered the closer you approach it, as argued in Wordsworth's 'Immortality Ode'. Birth or conception aspired to retrospectively looks more like the impoverishment or end of life. *Alastor*'s poet closes on his own sources only to discover 'Nature's... cradle, and his sepulchre' (l. 430).

His quest, though, is also an exercise in comparative cultural history. Like influential contemporaries, from Sir William Jones to A. W. Schlegel, he searches for the Indo-European matrix of Western civilization, wandering through the ruins of Athens, Tyre, Balbec, Babylon, Memphis, and Thebes. Then, as if following the map written by Coleridge's poem 'Kubla Khan', he journeys on to the source of the great rivers nourishing those cultural centres – Nile, Indus, Oxus, and eventually some composite torrent he pursues to its mountain spring in another moment of conception barren of instruction. While this learning has its radical dimension, placing Christian civilization in humbling perspective, it is also represented as being as abortive as the psychological quest. Shelley's poem encourages our post-colonial interpretation of Romantic orientalism as a mode of imperialism that aims finally to uncover not something different, but the same. The orientalist studies his own reflection rather than another form of life. He recognizes not a set of irreducibly different values and practices, but his own civilization in a primitive, exotic infancy, aesthetically superior, perhaps, but as yet only having the potential to reach current levels of enlightenment.

In *Alastor*, Shelley immerses himself in a prevailing Romantic idiom, poetic, ethnic, and philosophical. He does so critically, though, exposing its limitations from within. The poet's perpetual soliloquy – keeping 'mute conference/With his still soul' (ll. 223–4) – dissolves rather than assures personal identity. In this Humean theatre of impressions, no idea of the self leaps forward for the poet's use. The disconcerted philosopher stands beside the orgasmic poet. Shelley locates mistaken expectations of fixed identity in the poetic self-images of Wordsworth and Coleridge, criticizing their pretensions to universality by valuing them as voices of their time. When, for example, the poet cries to the stream bearing him towards his goal, 'Thou imagest my life'

(l. 505), he is both right and wrong, right in his identification with unending process, wrong to think that such identification defines individuality. Another companion poem in the *Alastor* volume, 'Mutability' (R&P 88), stresses the hopelessness of clinging to the idea of a unique self persisting unchanged through time. When a mountaineer encounters *Alastor*'s poet 'on some dizzy precipice', he sees a 'spectral form' and thinks 'that the Spirit of wind . . . had paused/In its career' (ll. 257–62). This exciting arrestation, for all its personifying power, is very different from the image of a mind dissolved in others' responses to it, the life of poetic creativity heroically endorsed in Shelley's 'Ode to the West Wind' (R&P 221–3).

Like his contemporary the philosopher Hegel, Shelley thought that the idea of sameness is contradictory: we only remain the same by changing in characteristic ways; our individuality is an unfinished dialectic of same and other, a reciprocal affair enhanced through association in its broadest sense. Extrapolating from the individual case, one can say that Shelley thinks that any establishment artificially arrests this mutual formation: to insist on the same at the expense of the other fosters a tyranny stunting both. In just one sonnet, 'Feelings of a Republican on the Fall of Bonaparte' (M&E 455–6), he can therefore switch, with an ease shocking at the time, from condemning Napoleonic imperialism to attacking the established constitutionalism which defeated it – 'Old Custom, legal Crime,/And bloody Faith the foulest birth of time' (ll. 13–14). Fortunately, Time is no vegetarian and devours its own progeny. Unfortunately, Shelley is as much Time's victim as his enemies. In *Queen Mab*, Mab calls on Time to 'Render thou up thy half-devoured babes' for the edification of Ianthe (VIII. 5). Shelley sets no limits to our powers of sympathetic reconstruction, provided they are historical not transcendental, recoveries we are as much subject to as subjects of. The 'fructifying virtue' Wordsworth first attributed to 'spots of time' in 1799 is, for Shelley, a growth beyond personal control. He opposes all transcendental self-regard, aesthetic or national, with an openness to new associations that continually reform both private and political life, relationship and citizenship.

4

Hyper-reality

In the summer of 1816 Shelley wrote two extraordinary poems, 'Hymn to Intellectual Beauty' (M&E 522–32) and 'Mont Blanc' (M&E 532–49). 'Hymn' and 'Mont Blanc' are now known to have existed in at least two main manuscript versions, the ones used for publication (the B-texts in the citations that follow) and others written earlier in a notebook entrusted for return to England to Byron's friend, Scrope Davies (the A-texts). Scrope Davies then appears to have mislaid the notebook, which was unearthed from a Pall Mall vault of Barclays bank in 1976. Place, predictably, greatly influenced the creativity of a poet fascinated by affinities between his inner and outer life, and by the exemplary association they represented for society and politics. By June 1816 Shelley, Mary Godwin, and their new baby, William, found themselves living by Lake Geneva, just below the Villa Diodati, once briefly stayed in by Milton and now occupied by Byron. The memory of Alpine scenery from his six weeks' continental tour with Mary in 1814 had partly energized the landscapes of *Alastor*, and poetically exaggerated the riverscapes around Bishopsgate, near Windsor, where it was written. Now it surrounded him. He and Byron were quickly on friendly enough terms to plan a circumnavigation of the lake on which they enjoyed stormy dangers together and paid homage at Clarens and Lausanne to Rousseau and Gibbon respectively. Clarens, scene of Rousseau's *La Nouvelle Héloise*, was of more importance to Shelley than the house at Lausanne where in the 1780s Gibbon had finished his admirably (to Shelley's mind) anti-Christian *The History of the Decline and Fall of the Roman Empire*. A later expedition to Chamonix, without Byron this time, inspired the topographical response called 'Mont Blanc'. But 'A Hymn' is thought to have been conceived on the boat-trip with the other poet, a journey on which Shelley spent much of the time reading *La Nouvelle Héloise*. He wrote letters to Peacock describing both outings and claimed that it was on the earlier voyage that he 'first knew the divine beauty of Rousseau's imagination', which came from 'a mind so powerfully bright as to cast a shade of falsehood on the records that are called reality' (*Letters*, i. 480, 485).

'Hymn to Intellectual Beauty' and 'Mont Blanc' complement each other when, inspired by Rousseau, they search for a kind of hyper-reality, source both of the world and of our interpretations of it. If we believe our interpretations of reality to be definitive, we traduce what both poems call a 'power'. To take that power's temporary expression through an aspect of reality for the whole of reality is to produce ideology. By writing poetry evocative of the power to produce but then exceed these convenient compromises, Shelley once more links scientific and political scepticism. He exposes the provisional character of any ideological settlement on the nature of things that passes itself off as final: 'the name of God, and ghosts, and Heaven,/Remain the records of [that] vain endeavour' ('Hymn', B., ll. 27–9). We must accept that 'Power dwells apart' ('Mont Blanc', B., l. 96). And though the effort to define something so 'Remote, serene and inaccessible' ('Mont Blanc', B., l. 97) might appear hopeless, this exercise in dissatisfaction raises the more important hope that its obscure object of desire will 'free/This world from its dark slavery' ('Hymn', B., l. 70). Hence Mont Blanc's otherwise startling political articulacy: 'Thou hast a voice, great Mountain, to repeal/ Large codes of fraud and woe' ('Mont Blanc', B., l. 80–1).

While we can interleave themes common to the two poems in this way, their emphases are different. 'Hymn' criticizes the use of transcendental categories to close down the possibilities of reality; 'Mont Blanc' grapples more directly with the open-ended thing itself. 'Hymn' recalls the eighteenth-century latitude allowing hymns to celebrate not only religious subjects but also solitude, science, and the seasons. It also echoes the militantly anti-clerical hymns of French Revolutionary festivals, and, still further back, the pagan tradition from which Shelley later translated Homer's hymns to Mercury, the Moon, the Sun, and other divinities. Shelley's 'Hymn' is thus provocatively secular to his Christian culture; it also revives older ideas of the sacred by consecrating the response to natural beauty. This beauty is found in process: to be appreciated, it demands that we infer from effect to cause, enjoying the subtleties of connection involved: 'As summer winds that creep from flower to flower. –/Like moonbeams that behind some piny mountain shower' (B., ll. 4–5). That final verb, 'shower', proves too syntactically subtle for most first readers. The same troubling of our powers of causal inference is obvious in the 'Ode to the West Wind' (R&P 221–3). When we find the spring wind 'Driving sweet buds like flocks to feed in air' (l. 11), we have to switch codes of explanation to appreciate that now temperature, rather than motion, accounts for the wind's 'unseen presence' as its warmth excites buds to blossom, filling 'with living hues and odours plain and hill' (l. 12).

Wordsworth's *Excursion* would have already confirmed to Shelley that Wordsworth understood possession by natural beauty as preparation for citizenship in a Christian society. Shelley's worship of natural beauty, by contrast, is intellectually engaged by the 'Doubt, chance, and mutability' ('Hymn', B., l. 31) institutional religion seeks to dispel. The narrator of 'Hymn' also accepts a corresponding inner instability: 'Love, Hope and Self-esteem, like clouds depart/And come, for some uncertain moments lent' (B., ll. 37–8). The poem assuages those miseries, but not, in the manner of Wordsworth's 'Tintern Abbey' or 'Immortality Ode', by finding in the diminished presence of nature improved powers – 'the philosophic mind' – to represent it, symbolic skills which then socialize the communicative adult. When Shelley hymns 'The awful shadow of some unseen Power' (B. l. 1), he appears to share with Wordsworth the same Platonic understanding of representation: 'shadow' would then signify the failure adequately to represent an original. Epistemological weakness leaves us with shadows of the truth, only compensated for by the philosophical knowledge of that weakness and of the best society for regulating it. But, in another, Lucretian tradition, the shadow is rather a further perfection of the original, a sign of its productivity and increase rather than its pale imitation. Poetry of this temper will, therefore, participate in an endless creativity, not record with symbolic pathos its separation from it.

Comparison of the two versions of 'Hymn' shows that Shelley thought 'Spirit' to be synonymous with or to clarify 'Shadow'.

The 'Shadow of Beauty' (A., l. 13) opening stanza 2 in Scrope Davies becomes 'Spirit of BEAUTY' (B., l. 13) in the version used by Leigh Hunt for the poem's first publication in the *Examiner* of January 1817. 'Spirit', for 'Shadow', emphasizes an agency in reflection, as when we reflect upon some topic. This 'intellectual' dimension, in other words, connects the 'beauty' described in the poem to a circuit of activity. The poem then is self-identical with its subject: it is not the impoverished semblance of it, inviting a Wordsworthian resignation to what remains, but another example of it in action. The mutability to which 'intellectual beauty' can give 'grace and truth' finally provokes in the poet a humanitarian love liberated from ideology. The same logic stimulates a 'fear' of 'himself'. The word 'fear' strives to mean only 'respect' but cannot, in context, suppress an anxiety at the next change towards which the poem's last, autumnal stanza directs him.

> The day becomes more solemn and serene
> When noon is past – there is a harmony
> In autumn, and a lustre in its sky,
> Which through the summer is not heard or seen,
> As if it could not be, as if it had not been!
> Thus let thy power, which like the truth
> Of nature on my passive youth
> Descended, to my onward life supply
> Its calm – to one who worships thee,
> And every form containing thee,
> Whom, SPIRIT fair, thy spells did bind
> To fear himself, and love all human kind.
>
> (B., ll. 73–84)

'Mont Blanc' spectacularly elaborates on the difficulties of identifying with a power to change all our ideological preconceptions. Formally, the strictly ordered rhyme scheme of 'A Hymn' gives way to artful irregularity. Semantically, the poem makes it hard to distinguish mental from material categories, as when in the first stanza 'The source of human thought its tribute brings/Of waters' (B., ll. 5–6). The mountain seems capable of framing both the poet's mind and its external object, somehow figuring a reality productive of both. What appears absolute to us could therefore have been different. We view a scene 'Where Power in likeness of the Arve comes down/

From the ice gulfs that gird his secret throne' (B., ll. 16–17). Power might take another form. Viewing Mont Blanc, 'I seem.../to muse on my own separate fantasy', a fantasy that includes its own supposedly external corrective, 'the clear universe of things around'. Evaporated into a 'legion of wild thoughts', this universe floats detached from Mont Blanc's hyper-reality (B., ll. 35–41). Paradoxically, poetic projections are needed to evoke the substance that has rendered the literal universe insubstantial.

Many critics have given up here, pronouncing such extraordinarily interactive metaphors, which so freely swop literal and figurative dimensions, to be plainly incoherent. F. R. Leavis's is perhaps the most famous condemnation: 'a general tendency of the images to forget the status of the metaphor or simile that introduced them and to assume an autonomy and a right to propagate.'[1]

> The everlasting universe of things
> Flows through the mind, and rolls its rapid waves,
> Now dark – now glittering – now reflecting gloom –
> Now lending splendour, where from secret springs
> The source of human thought its tribute brings
> Of waters, – with a sound but half its own.
>
> ('Mont Blanc', B., ll. 1–6)

The difficulty of these lines comes from their bid to speak from behind or prior to normal ways of dividing up life into dominant subjects and passive objects. Leavis in fact describes reasonably accurately a mode of depicting reality which has persuasive philosophical advocates. From Adorno and Horkheimer's *Dialectic of Enlightenment* onwards, a cluster of theories with ecological leanings has favoured a polymorphic, assymetrical depiction of nature, one honouring primarily its resistance to technological control. Conversely, Shelley's visions have been aligned with the latest technologies of matter. In an article on 'The Quantum Mechanical Shelley', Arkady Plotinsky strikes a definitely Shelleyan chord with his description of 'quantum systems, defined by an irreducible, infinite multiplicity and incessant transformations of their elements'.[2] Lacking the theories of a Niels Bohr or Werner Heisenberg, Shelley has to express his pre-theoretical intuitions through those contemporary aesthetic and poetic idioms – such as 'the sublime' – that conventionally license exceptions to scientific understanding.[3] Yet 'Mont Blanc' stretches even this latitude to breaking point. The 'Preface' to *History of a Six Weeks' Tour*, where the poem was first published, asks for 'Mont Blanc' to be read 'as an undisciplined overflowing of the soul [which] rests its claim to approbation on an attempt to imitate the untameable wildness and inaccessible solemnity from which those feelings sprang'.[4] Can 'undisciplined overflowing' be justified aesthetically? Wordsworth described 'all good poetry' in his 'Preface' to *Lyrical Ballads* both as the 'spontaneous overflow of powerful feelings' and as 'emotion recollected in tranquility', the latter formula suggesting to Leavis a thoughtful, critical dimension lacking in Shelley's poetry. Wordsworth, though, in a remark proleptically countering Leavis, said that 'Shelley is one of the best *artists* of us all: I mean in workmanship of style'. Wordsworth's own poetic deference to our preconscious involvement with nature led him to write of 'a dark invisible workmanship'.[5] Shelley's obscurity, where it derives from efforts to figure a nature unmediated by ideology, appears to enjoy Wordsworthian sanction.

In other words, to be 'undisciplined' need not preclude Shelley's English from being what Leavis called 'a discipline of thought'.[6] But the rules of this discipline are observed in eluding what we normally mean by a discipline or the appearance of systematic understanding. Hence its difficulty. This project, however, has good philosophic precedent. In his letter to Peacock describing the Alpine extremes on the road to Chamonix, Shelley claims that 'All was as much our own as if we had been the creators of such impressions in the minds of others, as now occupied our own – Nature was the poet' (*Letters*, i. 497). Again, we see him trying to fashion a position from which he can see his mind and the objects of its knowledge as themselves the products of a hyper-reality. The subject is placed within the process of its own natural production and so cannot be said to represent or circumscribe it from the outside. Hence the subject reflecting on landscape must abdicate its own sovereignty to disclose what underwrites them both. In Romantic philosophy from Kant to Schelling, such a simultaneous grasp of conscious and unconscious activity is possible only in art, in the form of Shelley's 'as if we had been the creators . . .'. The effect on poetic language of this ambition is, as Isobel Armstrong put it, 'to dissolve priority and dependence by achieving a perfect reciprocity of identity, exchange and difference. Things merge into another's being and maintain their being.'[7] This language gives with one hand and takes away with the other. The poem is about the power to produce the things it describes, including itself. Its objects, therefore, all illustrate each other's origins to some extent, but the poem must surrender credit for that power of illustration to the same source.

> there, many a precipice,
> Frost and the Sun in scorn of mortal power
> Have piled: dome, pyramid, and pinnacle,
> A city of death, distinct with many a tower
> And wall impregnable of beaming ice.
> Yet not a city, but a flood of ruin
> Is there, that from the boundaries of the sky
> Rolls its perpetual stream.
>
> (B., ll. 102–9)

Descriptions settle for a second, then are shrugged off by the onward motion they had momentarily fixed. But a sense of that motion takes shape in, not outside, this process. The energy of glaciers is to be caught in the series of endless approximations that language both describes and suffers.

The poem's enigmatic conclusion – 'And what wert thou, and earth, and stars, and sea,/If to the human mind's imaginings / Silence and solitude were vacancy?' (B., ll. 142–4) – suggests that our world is inevitably diminished if we cannot relinquish the claim to be its authoritarian subject. To abdicate ideological sovereignty, though, may be unthinkable. Silence, solitude and/or vacancy must become positive terms if we are to imagine a thoroughgoing liberation from prejudice and vested interest. The poem's ending makes the proto-Marxian admission that to question our cultural ideas of autonomy must at least *appear* to us like the questioning of freedom altogether. On the other hand, the great precursor of Romantic attempts to escape self-interest and see things *sub specie aeternitatis* is Spinoza. And Spinoza thought that, in so far as we understand eternity, we feel 'intellectual love', a 'pleasure' that accompanies this perfection of our understanding. Spinozism is very different from the proselytizing Christianity with which Coleridge had imagined himself greeting the sunrise over Mont Blanc in 1802. His 'Hymn before Sun-Rise, in the Vale of Chamouni', to which Shelley's 'Mont Blanc' must be a riposte, celebrates Legitimacy by having the same mountain, 'Great Hierarch', tell 'the silent sky,/And tell the stars, and tell yon rising sun/Earth, with her thousand voices, praises GOD.'[8] Spinoza's view, that our self-understanding and emotional well-being are interchangeable with the adequacy of our idea of nature, supports the challenging impersonality precipitated in the language of 'Mont Blanc'.

We are not all philosophers of Spinoza's degree of single-mindedness. We negotiate our ideas of greater freedom and a better life by stages, in dialogue, and through practical compromises with each other. Our aspirations may be finally rationalized by the inexorable logic of Spinoza's *Ethics* and Shelley's 'Mont Blanc'. Shelley's subsequent work, though, displays less taxing expectations of his audience, though he never popularizes his ideas enough for his critical friend, Peacock. The ambition of figuring poetically an area beyond ideology, and confronting the contradictions and impasses involved, remains a perpetual undercurrent in Shelley's work, finally dominant in *The Triumph of Life* (R&P 453–70). A more dialogic approach is noticeable elsewhere: explicitly in 'Julian and Maddalo' (R&P 112–27) and the poetic dramas, implicitly from the historical commentary of *Laon and Cythna* (Rogers, 99–273) to the conversations of the last poems to Jane Williams. The year 1816 became one of shocking extremes for Shelley. His first wife, Harriet, and Fanny Imlay, the half-sister of his partner, Mary Godwin, both committed suicide. He befriended the most celebrated English poet of the age, Byron, but also had to start coping with the consequences of Byron's fling with Claire Clairmont. He married Mary in December, but perhaps partly in an attempt to forestall the attempt by Harriet's family to deny him custody of his and Harriet's children. All his battles within the ideological arena, though, were to make heard that voice beyond ideology, that power that 'dwells apart'.

5

Eros and Civilization

Just over a year after their time together at the Lake of Geneva, Shelley wrote to Byron that he 'had, completed a poem . . . in the style, and for the same object as "Queen Mab", but interwoven with a story of human passion' (*Letters*, i. 557). In this first apology for *Laon and Cythna* (Rogers, 99–273), he overlooks the achievment of 'Hymn' and 'Mont Blanc' to ask for his new 'vision of the nineteenth century' to be understood as a revision of his earlier 'Philosophical Poem', as he described *Queen Mab* to Byron. The new work is meant to improve on the language and connectedness of *Queen Mab*. Byron, unimpressed, declared that the poem's obscurity made it unnecessary for it to have been withdrawn, bowdlerized, and reissued as *The Revolt of Islam* (H&M 32–158). Shelley's 'Preface', though, describes the poem as 'an experiment on the temper of the public mind', recalling Wordsworth's claim almost twenty years earlier in his 'Advertisement' to *Lyrical Ballads*. Had he known, Shelley could also have been reviving the Coleridgean project of Wordsworth's unpublished *Prelude* to restore confidence in 'visionary minds'. Once more he resisted the fall into the religiosity and imperialism of the *Excursion*.

The 'Preface' describes the poetry of *Laon and Cythna* in language used by the later *A Defence of Poetry*. Here is little of the dramatic tension between poetic theory and performance found in *Alastor*. Shelley is ambitious of producing 'Poetry in its most comprehensive sense' (Rogers, 103). Shelley continues to widen the definition of poetry throughout his career. The state of mind of which, he told Godwin, his poem was a 'picture', attempted to use poetry to awaken a reciprocal sense of unregulated possibility in his readers (*Letters*, i. 577). Shelley hopes to receive confirmation of his own generously imagined state of mind from the 'enlightened and refined' (Rogers, 99). His élitism is not straightforward. His audience's enlightenment and refinement are functions of their poetic sympathy, and so designate membership of that disposable vanguard that extends through revolutionary thought from Marx to Lenin and Gramsci. In stating his affiliation to a culturally privileged class, Shelley redescribed that culture as a philanthropic capacity to think one's way beyond immediate interests – even, frightening paradox, at the cost of these cultural advantages that made such benevolence possible. Once more he envisages the radical forgetting of individuality, a 'Lethean joy' (V. 2090), in the creation of a larger identity.

The poem opens with a spectacular conflict, a dramatization of the implication of good in evil, beyond the power of *Queen Mab*'s outrage to discriminate. Here, on a stage lit by extraordinary meteorological pyrotechnics, appear 'an Eagle and a Serpent wreathed in fight' (I. 193). Their struggle appears internecine and ends with the 'lifeless' snake dropping into the ocean. But the serpent survives, swims to shore, and is nurtured by a 'Lady' who reveals to the watching narrator that, contrary to prejudice, the reptile represents good, 'though in the likeness of a loathed worm' (I. 398). This education of the narrator is the first of a series of scenes of instruction throughout the poem that attempt to release characters from their ideological preconceptions. An extreme example is the little child born of the rape of Cythna by the tyrant Othman who in life remains loyal to her father because she does not know 'what such change might be' to disown him (V. 1962). She cannot break such strongly binding kinship until she can enjoy an afterlife with her mother and Laon.

The Lady's initial explanation of the contest of eagle and serpent distils an extravagant Zoroastrian metaphysic of good and evil. Concocted mostly from the writings on vegetarianism of John Newton, and from mythological interests shared with Peacock, such speculation mixes with hard-headed pragmatism. The poem focuses our interest on 'what life, what power was kindled' by the fight as much as on its outcome. Excitement at the contest betrays our stake in the power common to the 'two Powers', one good one evil, that rule the universe. With this common power each shapes the other, making the definition of good and evil into a creative dynamic in which we participate, not a series of static ethical positions we can learn by rote. Later in the poem, the snake does stand for evils – 'Faith, an obscene worm' and 'Hate' (V. 2168; VIII. 3379). And 'bondage' can mean either the good effects of innovative communication or the customs standing in its way – free love or marriage (V. 2230). Common to both meanings is their creative response to different circumstances. In other words, we find pictured for us the *historical* character of our ideas. Our moral task is represented as a fight against evil, of which a continuing part is to undo the distorted shape to which good has grown under evil influence. Success, though, only gives evil a new image to corrupt prior to the next reformulation of the good.

Shelley historicizes his own idealism. Commitment to revolutionary social and political change is obliged to be utopian because its only recent practical example, the French Revolution, failed. Equally, it is just such a 'defect of correspondence' between ideas and reality that, the Preface claims, doomed the French Revolution to failure. The 'beau ideal of the French Revolution', which Shelley claims his poem to draw, can therefore only show, as Paul Dawson has described it, 'how a revolution which cannot achieve its aims ought to be conducted'.[1] Shelley's poem exposes simultaneously the weaknesses of a revolution forced to remain poetic, and the comprehensiveness of change, only expressible in poetry, to which revolution ought to aspire. Once more we enter the politics of imagined communities. The poem was originally withdrawn to edit out the incestuous relationship between Laon and Cythna. Their incest set them apart as each other's ideal audience and broke social taboos Shelley thought indefensible. The couple's highly wrought poetic intercourse with each other distances them from others but also serves the poem's claims to be an experimental communication, a thoroughgoing critique of existing institutions limiting social interchange. The narrator has to be conducted to the 'Temple of the Spirit' (XII. 4815) in order to hear the couple's exemplary story told – an imagined point of vantage recalling the artifice of *Queen Mab*'s chariot. But the belief that communication *can* constitute an alternative social fabric is the poem's most optimistic thesis.

Laon and Cynthia frequently describes language as a 'woof', the product of a kind of social weaving. After the defeat of Othman, the revolutionary victors enjoy 'a sacred festival,/A rite to attest the equality of all'. This reworking of the festivals with which the French Revolution temporarily replaced religious ceremony figures a new discourse in which people can relate to each other from different social positions.

> Over the plain the throngs were scattered then
>   In groups around the fires, which from the sea
> Even to the gorge of the first mountain-glen
>   Blazed wide and far; the banquet of the free
> Was spread beneath many a dark cypress-tree,
> Beneath whose spires, which swayed in the red flame,
>   Reclining, as they ate, of Liberty,
> And Hope, and Justice, and Laone's name,
> Earth's children did a woof of happy converse frame.
>
> (V. 2290–8)

Certain ideals are part-embodied in their own communication. They become a texture, a fabric, a material whose pattern is made up of everyone's contributions, their 'converse'; which is to say that the meaning of Liberty, Hope, and Justice lies in their communal production.

Reunited in the festival, Cythna and Laon are found 'Weaving swift language from impassioned themes' (V. 2336). One of those is the tale of Cythna's solitary confinement, imprisoned by Othman in a roofless sea cave. Even then she could still find in language a pattern of the collaborative community from which she had been cut off. Her isolation empowers her to recognize what language is capable of: 'time imparted/Such power to me' (VII. 3094). In remembering uses of language, such as Laon's songs, she can say 'My mind became the book through which I grew/Wise in all human wisdom'. Where her isolation makes impossible the use of language to denote objects, she has to treasure its inner texture of relationships, and draw up signs of this linguistic interior.

> 'My mind became the book through which I grew
>   Wise in all human wisdom, and its cave,
> Which like a mine I rifled through and through,
>   To me the keeping of its secrets gave –
>   One mind, the type of all, the moveless wave
> Whose calm reflects all moving things that are:

Necessity, and love, and life, the grave
And sympathy (fountains of hope and fear),
Justice, and truth, and time, and the world's natural sphere.

'And on the sand would I make signs to range
These woofs, as they were woven, of my thought;
Clear, elemental shapes, whose smallest change
A subtler language within language wrought:
The key of truths which once were dimly taught
In old Crotona; – and sweet melodies
Of love, in that lorn solitude I caught
From mine own voice in dream, when thy dear eyes
Shone through my sleep, and did that utterance harmonize.

(VII. 3100–17)

The two stanzas are nicely poised between picturing an arcane lore of elemental archetypes or their perpetually mobile relationships. Crotona was the home of Pythagoras, vegetarian philosopher of deeper, numerological patterns underlying surface meanings. In fact the two pictures merge: the wave's 'moveless' mirror, image of the 'One mind, the type of all' (VII. 3104), is only a stage in its historical progression towards the shore. Just as her mind's cave displaces the cave in which Cythna is dungeoned, so her language refines on ordinary usage to distil a subtler sense of all the metaphorical connections with which we use language to bring us together in different relationships.

Shelleyan sympathy has its limits. The revolt led by Laon and Cythna specifically targets Eastern despotism. Is this choice explained by reference to the Ottoman Empire, denounced at the time by all philhellenes? Their cause is meant, transparently, to become Islam's – its 'revolt', not a revolt against it. Or are Othman and his crew the construction of a contemporary orientalism little different from the ideology of empire supposedly being execrated? Moral rehabilitation, some post-colonial critics have argued, could be as contemptuous of cultural difference as were cynical exploitation and military imperialism. Fairer redistribution of political and economic power also homogenizes so effectively those being reformed that it becomes difficult to decide which concern has been uppermost – justice or cultural uniformitarianism. Laon and Cythna are both Greeks from Argolis. The liberating songs of the young Laon aim either to foster democratic association or to colonize others with Western ideas of Enlightenment, depending on how we construe 'a bondage of such sympathy' (II. 803). As in some Romantic philosophy's Fichtean treatment of nature, the East becomes a field for moral action without regard to whether or not it might possess laws, standards, and customs themselves entitled to respect. Any thought of them is overwhelmed by vulgarly assimilating complex civilizations to crude religious stereotypes, easily dismissed. Or, as we saw exposed in *Alastor*, a nostalgia for exotic originals is superseded by what Hegel called 'real cultural progress'.[2] Arguably, just such moral confidence was to sustain later talk of the white man's burden. The difference from Shelley's orientalism must rest precariously in his tortured acceptance of a political ideal that would eclipse his own cultural heritage as surely as any other. Certainly that future remains a poetic possibility. But Shelley then looks set to lose the communicative dimension that elsewhere roots his ideals in social practice. His *Revolt* cannot envisage a multicultural resolution, hybrid and dialogical, between the West and Islam. They apparently cannot belong to the same textual fabric or history of the spirit.

Less apocalyptically, the poem's feminism tries to imagine a reformation in sexual relations: '"Can man be free if woman be a slave?"' (II. 1045). The heterosexual arena is a theatre of war:

> Never will peace and human nature meet
> Till free and equal man and woman greet
> Domestic peace.
>
> (II. 994–6)

In Canto VIII, Cythna preaches to her slaver captors feminist values of self-determination whose vulnerability would undermine everyone's security. Nevertheless, her apotheosis repeats the self-destructive logic by which Shelleyan sympathy escapes its own vested interests. As 'the prophetess of Love' (IX. 3641), she anticipates the poet of the 'Ode to the West Wind': 'Behold! Spring comes, though we must pass, who made/The promise of its birth' (IX. 3688–9). Although verging on the platitudinous, her apothegm is transfigured by the desperate lines that follow and heroically try to reverse the sententious meaning of the shadow of death. Wilfully reorientated, the shadow's length indicates not the setting sun but the rising sun, which casts longer shadows in the early morning:

> even as the shade
> Which from our death, as from a mountain, flings
> The future, a broad sunrise; thus arrayed
> As with the plumes of overshadowing wings,
> From its dark gulf of chains, Earth like an eagle springs.
>
> (IX. 3689–93)

The future does the flinging, but how hard the reader has to work on the stylistic inversions to wring this optimistic meaning from the verse!

This moralizing wants to take us by surprise. The immortality figured here by Cythna to her lover, though, takes place not historically, but in history, in the memory of others. Bodily decomposition is transposed into 'Calumny', to be outlived by 'fame' and 'human hope':

> 'And Calumny meanwhile shall feed on us,
> As worms devour the dead, and near the throne
> And at the altar, most accepted thus
> Shall sneers and curses be; – what we have done
> None shall dare vouch, though it be truly known;
> That record shall remain, when they must pass
> Who built their pride on its oblivion;
> And fame, in human hope which sculptured was,
> Survive the perished scrolls of unenduring brass.
>
> (IX. 3739–47)

Cythna tries to persuade us that all our individual fears can be discounted if we are in tune with historical progress and necessity. What might have convinced as a Renaissance conceit true only to the exaggerated confidence of erotic love (and the poem features a Romantic *Liebestod* as well) is here given as a law for all. Paradoxically, by sharing their fame, sculpting it out of our 'human hope', Laon and Cythna make their optimism appear even more peremptory and unlikely than that of the singular lovers of Shakespeare's sonnets or Donne's songs and elegies.

Once more, aspirations towards a Lucretian equanimity in the face of death – and the doctrines of *De rerum natura* 'are yet the basis of our metaphysical knowledge' according to the 'Preface'

– furnish words for the kind of revolutionary selflessness *Laon and Cynthia* endorses. The poem's linguistic difficulties arise from its expression of the open-endedness of its own patterning, exceeding the personal control of the speaker in the production of better modes of living:

> 'Virtue, and Hope, and Love, like light and Heaven,
> Surround the world. – We are their chosen slaves.
> Has not the whirlwind of our spirit driven
> Truth's deathless germs to thought's remotest caves?
>
> (IX. 3667–70)

The agony of such successful self-dissemination is subliminally acknowledged:

> let those who come
> Behind, for whom our steadfast will has bought
> A calm inheritance, a glorious doom,
> Insult with careless tread our undivided tomb!
>
> (IX. 3726–9)

'Insult' here surely intensifies an etymological meaning of jumping or leaping over the tomb into an image of insupportable superiority. Cythna, lovingly importuning Laon, rewords Shelley's philosophical and political crux.

6

Communicative Action

In March 1818 Shelley set off for Italy never again to return to England. Thereafter, his life was constitutionally unsettled, a patchwork of moves to and removals from houses in Pisa, Lucca, Livorno, Rome, Naples, Venice, and elsewhere. He began writing *Prometheus Unbound* (R&P 130–210) in a summer house at Este. He continued composing it the following spring, writing Acts II and III among the ruins of the Roman baths of Caracalla. The picture of a Romantic poet alone with his vision amid the relics of a glorious past is irresistibly Romantic. Shelley's own attitude towards the poem was indulgent. He frequently called it his 'favourite', written for the few or the 'elect' like *Laon and Cythna*. The death of Clara Shelley, aged 1, after his mismanagement of medication and travel, and his consequent estrangement from Mary, would have enforced his isolation. Act IV was written after the second hammer-blow of the death of the 3½-year-old William Shelley. Perhaps such misery might also have stimulated a compensatory extremism of creativity. He told Peacock in April 1819 that he had now finished 'a drama, with characters & mechanism of a kind yet unattempted' (*Letters*, ii. 94). Echoing Milton, Shelley used his classical model, Aeschylus' play *Prometheus Bound*, as a foil for his fiercely revisionist effort.[1]

By the time he writes its 'Preface', though, Shelley is busy assimilating his lyrical drama to a consistent poetic practice. Other shorter poems of the same time, like the fragmentary 'A Vision of the Sea' (H&M 596–600), harbour more directly therapeutic content; impossibly, 'A Vision' sustains a final image of mother and child above a shipwreck before itself falling prematurely silent, expressively deferring, perhaps, to Mary's own withdrawal. *Prometheus Unbound*, though, is consistent with Shelley's 'purpose... hitherto... simply to familiarise the highly refined imagination of the more select classes of poetical readers with beautiful idealisms of moral excellence' (R&P 135). Shelley's Prometheus, unlike the escapee of Aeschylus' own lost *Prometheus Unbound*, is 'the type of the highest perfection of moral and intellectual nature' and reaches no pragmatic accommodation with his oppressor, Jupiter (R&P 133). But the most basic difficulty for Shelley's reader is less the learnedness of allusion than the hierarchy of characters. Again in the 'Preface' Shelley tells us not to look for 'a reasoned system'; the imagery he employs is 'in many instances ... drawn from the operations of the human mind, or from those external actions by which they are expressed' (R&P 133). He appears simultaneously to bar us from allegory and to invite us to read the poem allegorically. We encounter Gods, Titans, Spirits, shadows, hours, planets, a demiurge, mankind, fauns, elements, and continents inevitably suggesting different levels of representation. Our primary task as readers appears to be to gauge their degree of authenticity or closeness in figuring the human mind through idealization, parody, and symbol. On the other hand, the action of the play shows everything to be equally subject to necessity. But by reimagining the losses necessity imposes as one's own willed self-sacrifice, by making them one's own in a spirit of love, this levelling of distinction creates an enabling republic.

In the prose fragment 'On Life' (R&P 474–8), probably written around the time he was beginning to compose Act IV in late 1819, Shelley attacks popular distinctions between mind and matter and the philosophical preferences to which they give rise. *Prometheus Unbound* can perhaps be best understood as presenting an alternative to the traditional battle in the philosophical imagination between the claims of mind and body to originate or explain human experience. Stylistically, its mixture of lyric, drama, and epic marries Romantic freedom to classical form with similar impartiality. And it is an argument for such equivalences that it acts out, one directed against interpretations of knowledge or artistic success as the mastery of one thing by another. Prometheus does not champion humankind by representing it at a higher, divine court. Instead, his resistance to monarchic authority excites a 'great Republic' of self-governing individuals, a political configuration into which characters of all ranks gravitate in the final act (IV. 533).

How are they led to this conclusion? Act I opens with the Titan, Prometheus, bound to a precipice, trying to recall the curse he pronounced on his imprisoner, Jupiter. Prometheus' immortality, it turns out, is a limitation not an advantage in this exercise. For the curse to be repeated without bringing down Jupiter's wrath, it has to be uttered by a ghost or phantom from the world of the dead. As Prometheus' mother, the earth, describes it,

> there are two worlds of life and death:
> One that which thou beholdest, but the other
> Is underneath the grave, where do inhabit
> The shadows of all forms that think and live
> Till death unite them.
>
> (I. 195–9)

Now such a union, with its suggestion of the completion of otherwise partial individuals, is clearly denied to the undying Titan. The expected advantage of immortality over mortality is upset. Another, moral advantage disappears with the aptness with which the shadow of Jupiter, when summoned, delivers Prometheus' curse. Their bond comes from the self-defeating intimacy of mastery with the object it enslaves. Prometheus' curse invites Jupiter to do his worst. Its imagery suggests that Jupiter's tyranny is fixated by the abjection it inflicts; recognition of his ascendancy decreases in proportion to the subjection of his victim. His defeat will come when he is shown finally to have taken the place of his slave.

> An awful Image of calm power
> Though now thou sittest, let the hour
> Come, when thou must appear to be
> That which thou art internally.
> And after many a false and fruitless crime
> Scorn track thy lagging fall through boundless space and time.
>
> (I. 296–301)

But emancipation by this means traps the victorious slave in the same questionable ascendancy.

Hegel famously described the master–slave relationship as an immature stage in the production of our knowledge of the world. But Prometheus' masochism, prescribed by his curse, appears equally suspect, bound by the same limited horizons, fuelled by what Nietzsche was to call *ressentiment*, a delight in suffering he associated with Christianity. By contrast, for Nietzsche 'what is amazing about the religiosity of the ancient Greeks is the enormous abundance of gratitude it exudes'.[2] And 'gratitude', as Prometheus sees, is precisely what Jupiter's evil prevents him from feeling:

> He who is evil can receive no good;
> And for a world bestowed, or a friend lost,
> He can feel hate, fear, shame – not gratitude.
>
> (I. 389–91)

Inherent in mastery is this numbness to the gift of others: an inability to acknowledge a defining lack in oneself, which, according to Shelley's sketch 'On Love' (R&P 473–4), only others can complete. Mastery further fixes the self within rigid boundaries stunting its development. When the Furies torture Prometheus, they do so by recounting human history to him in a way that suggests it to be an inalienable autobiography, the nightmare from which you can never awake. The Fury's final twist of the knife is to describe history as peopled by those who 'dare not devise good for man's estate/And yet they know not that they do not dare' (I. 623–4). Worse than the dismal history of atrocities is the perpetrators' demeaning ignorance of anything better than to be on the winning side. Fear of other modes of relationship locks master and slave into a cycle of exploiter and exploited.

Prometheus revokes his curse and breaks the pattern of domination. Other leading figures in the action, Demogorgon and Asia, also replace the master–slave relationship with those motivated by necessity and love. When these two forces come together, Jupiter is unseated, Prometheus released, and a Promethean age of republicanism dawns. G. M. Matthews succinctly describes Shelley's scientific corroboration of this moral drama.

> The scientist James Hutton had recently explained how the earth recreated itself by perennial cycles of volcanic activity, and it was believed that eruptions were triggered off by the entry of water from the sea. So when Asia and her sea-sisters penetrate the mountain of Demogorgon, who is described as if he were made of molten lava, they activate an eruption out of which the old earth is reborn.[3]

On the level of myth, inspired by Hesiod and his followers rather than Hutton, Demogorgon is the son of Jupiter and will one day triumph over his father. Etymologically, Demogorgon's name also suggests the power of the people (demos) to petrify (gorgon-like) its opponents, exposing their rigid, obsolete identities. Asia, lover of Prometheus, has a diametrically opposite effect. 'Asia!', Prometheus says of her, 'who when my being overflowed/Wert like a golden chalice to bright wine' (I. 809–10). She can provoke, contain and return an increase in self as a fresh identity to be enjoyed. Eventually, as Panthea tells her, it is 'the whole world which seeks thy sympathy' (II. v. 34).

For love to become the cosmic principle might seem to revive a Christian cosmogony. Provocatively Shelley mobilizes metaphorically the love that moves sun and stars in Dante's universe, or that 'faire cheyne of love' that, Theseus tells us at the end of Chaucer's 'The Knight's Tale', providentially connects up everything. Earth's orbit paved by love, pattern of 'a happy Soul', is one of Demogorgon's culminating visions (IV. 519–22). Predictably, Shelley is trying to empty a tradition of its dogmatic pretensions to mastery in order to reveal its lasting poetic significance. The 'distorted notions' of Dante and Milton, we remember from Shelley's *A Defence of Poetry*, 'are merely the mask and the mantle' disguising their writing's typically poetic susceptibility to reinterpretation in other terms (R&P 498). It is this openness to eternity or continuous redefinition that the conversation at the heart of *Prometheus Unbound* between Demogorgon and Asia establishes.

Allowed to question Demogorgon as she likes, Asia fearlessly explores the origins of authority – 'Who reigns?' (II. iv. 32) Her quest unfolds a history replacing the cyclical tale of the Furies. Her great speech starts with the contradiction in Jupiter's mastery implied by Hesiod's *Theogony* and pursued by Aeschylus' *Prometheus Bound*:

> There was the Heaven and the Earth at first
> And Light and Love; – then Saturn, from whose throne
> Time fell, an envious shadow.
>
> (II. iv. 32–5)

Compressed here is the story in which Saturn, in Greek mythology called Kronos (time), emasculates his father the Sky but is supplanted in turn by his son, Jupiter. Jupiter will *in time* be deposed by his son, Demogorgon, who appears as the power of temporality redoubled. You cannot kill time off. The story is now about the impossibility of making into one of its characters the essentially temporal dimension of storytelling itself. Such authorial will to mastery is as contradictory as Jupiter's own attempt to make time stand still. Demogorgon, on the other hand, transcends individuality and is 'Fate, Time, Occasion, Chance, and Change' (II. iv. 119) – temporality in all its aspects. On a Freudian reading, Demogorgon is the Oedipal structure rather than an Oedipal character: the precondition for the possibility for any ego-formation at all, not a figure in the Greek story.

Asia remorselessly exposes the nonsense of Jupiter's authority, 'stripped of power...by his own foolish purposes', as Aeschylus' Prometheus predicts.[4] Jupiter is a slave by virtue of being a master. 'Who is his master? Is he too a slave?', asks Asia (II. iv. 109). The only escape from this infinite regress is to accept that, like the shapeless Demogorgon, 'the deep truth is imageless' (II. iv. 116), and cannot be understood in the way a subject knows or masters an object or individual. As in 'Mont Blanc', power dwells apart. A proper sympathy with power, in Wordsworthian phrase, is a rapport achieved through love. We must cultivate a sympathetic attitude that renounces selfishness or the (pre-Oedipal) idea that the world is at our disposal. Prometheus comes to realize (from the other side, as it were) that only through love can the mortal limitations of the self cease to be murderous: one's centre of gravity is, sympathetically, everywhere; one is no longer one thing to be killed, '[man] being, not what he is', the fragment 'On Life' claims, 'but what he has been, and shall be...This is the character of all life and being'(R&P 476).

Increasingly, in *Prometheus Unbound*, Shelley's language tries to be adequate to this generous conception. Men and women leave behind individual limitations to become heirs to an open-ended tradition. Their affiliation to what is characteristically human associates them with, rather than distances them from, other modes of life and being. Learning from Jupiter's mistake, they sympathize with all possibilities of their medium of existence, rather than try to limit it through utilitarian objectifications. They present a political and biological internationale, socially egalitarian and scientifically interactive. In Shelley's neologism, the earth has become 'intertranspicuous', surely the ultimate in sympathetic porousness (IV. 246)? Language is described as 'a perpetual Orphic song', spurring into communicative action 'a throng/Of thoughts and forms, which else senseless and shapeless were' (IV. 415–17). Like Orpheus, this language can inspire nature, and like the Orphic cults of ancient times it seeks out bodily sources of enlightenment. Its material harmonies displace semantics, foregrounding instead a lyric music like the music of the spheres – 'a sense of words upon my ear... A universal sound like words' (IV. 517–18). This grounding in poetic sympathy of ancient myths and obsolete astronomies makes good the promise of two outstanding lyrics at the end of Act II, the universal distillation of 'Life of Life! thy lips enkindle' (II. v. 48) and Asia's 'My soul is an enchanted Boat' (II. v. 72). The latter significantly ends with a replay of *Alastor*'s final reversal of life processes back through the moment of conception. There it ends in extinction, criticizing the poet's narcissistic self-mirroring in an exoticized Oriental landscape. Here the East, personified by Asia, runs history backwards through 'a diviner day', or 'resurrection of the dead', as the source in Plato's *The Statesman* (2716) suggests.

> We have past Age's icy caves,
> And Manhood's dark and tossing waves
> And Youth's smooth ocean, smiling to betray;
> Beyond the glassy gulphs we flee
> Of shadow-peopled Infancy,
> Through Death and Birth to a diviner day,
> A Paradise of vaulted bowers
> Lit by downward-gazing flowers...
>
> (II. v. 98–105)

Asia thus hymns a new beginning for history, anticipating a syncretic, Promethean age whose future even Plato could not have imagined – 'Equal, unclassed, tribeless and nationless' (III. iv. 195).

What sort of poem can meaningfully stage such ambitious revisionings? Clearly not one reliant on the psychological plausibility of individual characters. The expansion of each centre of sympathy to take in the circumference of things lets self-sacrifice figure collective salvation. The reviewer in the

London Magazine of June 1820 got it right when he called *Prometheus Unbound* a poem 'more completely the child of the *Time* than almost any other modern production: it seems immediately sprung from the throes of the great intellectual, political, and moral *labour* of nations'. It is a macrocosmic poem. The reviewer quotes in his support the Preface's lines about 'The cloud of mind... discharging its collective lightning'.[5] In *A Philosophical View of Reform* (Clark, 229–61), written just after *Prometheus Unbound*, Shelley envisages radical opinion-formers of his own age (Godwin, Hazlitt, Bentham, Hunt) advocating reform in petitions to Parliament, communicative action reflecting the political convergence of their diverse intellectual interests: like Demogorgon's, their collective voice 'would be Eternity warning Time' (Clark, 259).

But, for *Prometheus Unbound* to convince, there has to be an almost religious confidence in the power to transform individual loss into public good. Discharges of the 'collective mind' have to draw on 'the collective energy of the moral and material world' which, according to Shelley's 'Essay on Christianity' (Clark, 196–215), is how 'every poet' has conceived of God. Normally, poets and reformers like Jesus use rhetoric or the 'art of persuasion' to accommodate their meaning to their audience. An 'entire sincerity' would be self-defeatingly obscure (Clark, 200–2). But Demogorgon's 'indefiniteness' resists such compromises: his final lines highlight the resulting crisis in communication he has presented throughout *Prometheus Unbound*.

To suffer woes which Hope thinks infinite;
To forgive wrongs darker than Death or Night;
  To defy Power which seems Omnipotent;
To love, and bear; to hope, till Hope creates
From its own wreck the thing it contemplates;
  Neither to change nor falter nor repent:
This, like thy glory, Titan! is to be
Good, great and joyous, beautiful and free;
This is alone Life, Joy, Empire and Victory.

(IV. 570–8)

Quite how 'hope' keeps its meaning here is baffling. That a transformation rather than an obliteration of its significance awaits it is the poem's great article of faith. Aeschylus' Prometheus is generally thought to have reached an accommodation with Zeus in the lost sequels to his *Prometheus Bound*. Shelley's poem negotiates with a mutability that can bring down any establishment, tyrannical or liberal. Consistently, Shelley seems prepared to put even poetry in historical jeopardy. It was when he told Peacock in January 1819 that he had finished the first Act of *Prometheus Unbound* that Shelley also made the startling disclaimer already quoted: 'I consider Poetry very subordinate to moral & political science, & if I were well, certainly I should aspire to the latter' (*Letters*, ii. 71). And in the Preface, he sticks to his guns, projecting 'a systematic history of what appear to me to be the genuine elements of human society' as his life's work, and telling his opponents not to presume that he would 'take Aeschylus rather than Plato', the tragedian rather than the systematic philosopher, as his 'model' (R&P 135). The confidence that Shelley's poem wants us to have in the idea of individual loss translating into wider good is thus meant to work for discourses as well. Hence, in *A Defence of Poetry*, Plato is recovered as a poet 'essentially' (R&P 484), but within a new definition of poetry that includes the creation of just institutions, changes in scientific paradigms and 'revolutions in opinion' (R&P 485). The definition, in other words, under which Shelley champions poetry loses that 'more restricted sense' of the word that one might be forgiven for thinking could not be sensibly abandoned.

7

Casuistry

In the summer of 1819, between the writing of Acts III and IV of *Prometheus Unbound*, Shelley worked on *The Cenci* (R&P 236–301), a play in which he avoided, as he told his readers in the Preface, 'the introduction of what is commonly called mere poetry' (R&P 241). He thus reiterates his ambition of releasing poetry from its current, 'more restricted sense'. Partly as a result of Shelley's own remarks, his tragedy has often been taken to be the 'sad reality' his more idealistic poetry sublimated (R&P 237). But Shelley's interest in the transvaluations possible under poetic pressure establishes a sometimes overlooked continuity between both modes of writing. *The Cenci's* contribution to this debate is to stage a historical attempt to transform apparently immutable moral, religious, and political principles, rather as he will do later in 'The Mask of Anarchy' (R&P 301–11).

In the Preface, Shelley likens the difficulties of this task to those of 'casuistry'. Casuistry is the bending of principles to take account of particular circumstances in individual cases, or the conflict of duties that may complicate a straightforward act of judgement.[1] Casuistry, like sophistry, has a pejorative ring to it, although some modern philosophers have thought its flexibility exemplary – 'the goal of ethical investigation', G. E. Moore called it in *Principia ethica*.[2] The hero of *Prometheus Unbound* is intended to be unambiguously good, and so to contrast with Milton's Satan, whom we are tempted by 'a pernicious casuistry' to exonerate on grounds of God's extreme provocation (R&P 133). In the case of the sexually abused parricide, Beatrice Cenci, Shelley is fascinated by 'the restless and anatomizing casuistry with which men seek the justification of Beatrice, yet feel she has done what needs justification' (R&P 240). In the culminating trial scene, Beatrice gets Marzio, one of the assassins she has suborned, to declare that she is innocent of killing the father who raped her. Is Marzio right or wrong? Is he mesmerized by Beatrice's charismatic authority, or in command of 'a higher truth', as he says? (V. ii. 164). Shelley implies that Beatrice's 'dramatic character' forces her audience to plumb their power to grasp, in the senses of *A Defence of Poetry*, 'before unapprehended relations of things'. Does Beatrice's performance in court collapse into a reprehensible casuistry, or does she carry the day as a poetic exemplar of a better dispensation to come when her 'crime' will be redescribed and she will be exonerated? The excitement for the audience lies in judging between these two possibilities.

The prophetic effort described in *A Defence of Poetry* simultaneously reconceives the status quo: it 'imagines what we know' in such a way as to justify its own innovations and foreshadowings. It detects the casuistry covertly at work in upholding the establishment. Count Cenci at first appears an extraordinary monster, but the play's imagery and action progressively cast him as representative, not egregious. He mixes perversion and natural wastage, a sadist for whom 'invention palls' with age. What he desires is desire, the return of appetite. For that, he would do anything – 'I know not what' (I. i. 99–103). Cardinal Camillo, the recipient of these disclosures, thanks God he cannot believe in such depravity. However, the embarrassing continuity between Cenci's outrageousness and the Catholic, ecclesiastical imaginary will be one of the play's main ironies. The Preface prepares the reader to look for the interwovenness of Italian Catholicism with all aspects of life; its religiosity typically coexists with, rather than, as in 'a Protestant apprehension', distinguishes itself from, profanity. Shelley's play goes further than his Preface when it suggests that the core Judaeo-Christian myth of a self-replicating God who makes man in his own image consecrates the motives of tyrannical patriarchs like the incestuous Cenci. As in *The Cenci*'s Elizabethan and Jacobean models, wickedness attributed to Italian Catholics can disguise attacks on Christian institutions generally.

Like Kronos, Cenci devours his children and tries, impossibly, to impersonate all times of life – 'quick youth . . . manhood's purpose stern, / And age's firm, cold, subtle villainy' (I. iii. 173–5) – to facilitate his incestuous purpose. The play's imagery implies that the God who creates creatures in his 'own image comparably extinguishes or prescinds human development. Casuistry takes account of the individuality thus scanted by God's law. Cenci is regarded as God's scourge, his 'image upon earth' (II. i. 17); but the other characters seem equally incapable of distinguishing one father from another: heavenly, ecclesiastical, and domestic fathers unite in their patriarchal appeal to 'a father's holy name' (II. ii. 73). Camillo tells of the Pope's fear of weakening 'the paternal power,/Being, as 'twere, the shadow of his own' (II. ii. 55–6). This assumption is shared by Cenci, and the divine patronage of patriarchy is shown to bind father to father indiscriminately when Marzio explains why – like Macbeth in similar circumstances – he cannot kill his sleeping victim at his first attempt.

> And now my knife
> Touched the loose wrinkled throat, when the old man
> Stirred in his sleep, and said, 'God! hear, O, hear,
> A father's curse! What, art thou not our father?'
> And then he laughed. I knew it was the ghost
> Of my dead father speaking through his lips,
> And could not kill him.
>
> (IV. iii. 16–22)

But these complicities show patriarchy to be a mask for economic interests rather than the universal system of natural values it claims to be. In fact, as Beatrice's mother sees, Cenci's patriarchy glosses over 'gold, opinion, law and power' (III. i. 185); the same 'Gold/Has whispered silence to his Holiness' (II. ii. 68) and reinforced his solidarity with Beatrice's father. This means that Beatrice can call the bluff of patriarchy. It is not what it pretends to be. It is, as she tells Marzio, 'an equivocation' (IV. iii. 28), another word important to *Macbeth*.

The play, therefore, lets Beatrice say truthfully, 'I have no father' (III. i. 40); she has no relation who can vindicate his authority in terms other than gold, opinion, law, and power. Anatomized, patriarchy reveals itself to be nothing more than the mechanics of keeping the control of society in the hands of a few men. Orsino is the character who remarks on the Cenci family's 'trick' of 'self-anatomy' (II. ii. 110). He is especially sensitive to their demythologizing, because he is a quintessentially religious hypocrite, proclaiming God's goodness for ulterior motives. Forced by Beatrice to 'Shew a poor figure to [his] own self-esteem', he still finds it one to which he can 'grow half reconciled' (II. ii. 117–18). As his first mention of it makes clear, this self-anatomizing is not simply analytic reflection on a subject but a dissection uncovering the material basis of supposedly immaterial values, a way of thinking I have been arguing to be characteristic of Shelley himself. Beatrice's gaze, he says, can 'anatomize me nerve by nerve' (I. ii. 85). The Cenci family's scepticism, though, allows radically different kinds of authentic self-creation. One is Cenci's brazen identification with what analysis unveils. Rather than lose out in his own self-estimation like Orsino, he embraces his worst motives and makes a virtue of his megalomania. And, ironically, in so doing, he falls in with the patriarchal logic of the Judaeo-Christian founding myth of a 'great God,/Whose image upon earth a father is' (II. i. 16–17), as it is adopted by the play's Catholic hierarchy.

Out of the materials anatomizing lays bare, Beatrice tries to fashion a self altogether different from the one prescribed by patriarchy. In her case, though, the encounter with the basic components of the self, exposing their potential for radical reconstruction, results not from wilful self-indulgence but from violation by her father. Initially, this leaves her disabled, dumbfounded, incapable of articulating what has happened to her. Her rape is something 'without a name', 'expressionless', a deed that has 'no form', suffering that has 'no tongue' (III. i. 116, 214, 142). But she rises to the challenge of disablement and sets out heroically to transvalue received morality to reach beyond the corrupt version of good and evil she has inherited. From a different perspective, Beatrice's imaginative reverse can be interpreted positively. It speaks her insight into the 'imageless' but 'deep truth' of Demogorgon, countenancing transformations that might otherwise appear self-annihilating.

In this vein, Beatrice personifies the historicizing spirit of poetry Shelley champions in *A Defence of Poetry*. According to the Preface, Beatrice exceeds and relativizes the terms in which she stands condemned. These only impersonate her. 'The crimes and miseries in which she was an actor and a sufferer are as the mask and the mantle in which circumstances clothed her for her impersonation on the scene of the world' (R&P 242). Beatrice herself shares this sense of being 'clothed' by others, principally her father. She thinks she can make a 'holier plea', which reduces to disposable 'garments' the conventional morality of her times. Her final judgement on herself is of living 'ever holy and unstained', despite being 'wrapped in a strange cloud of crime and shame' (v. iv. 148–9). This is casuistry pushed to its limits. If it fails, it does so because, again as G. E. Moore describes, 'it is far too difficult a subject to be treated adequately in our present state of knowledge'.[3] It looks for future corroboration, which Shelley's play partly bestows. The play may vindicate her in so far as she is consistently casuistical, but it also registers those moments when transvaluation falls back into the idiom it supposedly surpasses. Then Beatrice does not break but confirms the image in the mirror that her father has constructed for her. She hardens her heart, as her father tells Camillo he had done at the play's opening. Like Cenci, she sees herself as God's agent, her 'speedy act the angel of his wrath' (v. iii. 114). These compromises with the evil she opposes are Beatrice's 'pernicious mistakes'; but, without them, as the Preface concedes, she 'would never have been a tragic character' (R&P 240).

This concession appears to shift the blame to tragedy itself. The strategically pointed allusions to *Macbeth* then represent not the derivativeness of so much Romantic tragedy but calculated cultural criticism. Only a morally reactionary genre would require such failings of its heroines. Perhaps Shelley himself is being casuistical, using the restrictions of tragic heroism to historicize Beatrice's aspirations, showing that they belong to a particular culture at a particular time. Tragedy is their historically limited presentation against which Shelley's more adequate expression strives, as does his mythopoeia against Aeschylus in *Prometheus Unbound*. Beatrice's agon would then suggest another conclusion more in keeping with her intermittent figuring of Shelley's idea of poetry. Camillo, unwilling to have her tortured, calls her 'that most perfect image of God's love' (v. ii. 67). The terrible irony here is that on either interpretation, historicized or transvalued, she must perish. Either she is as bad as Cenci and the murderous patriarchy, which at that time lay claim to embody God's love. Or else she represents a fulfilment still to come, still unacknowledged, and so must expect execution under the prevailing regime.

8

Love's Work

Other poems produced by Shelley around the *annus mirabilis* in which most of *Prometheus Unbound* and *The Cenci* were written continue his quarrel with historical prescriptions of individual worth. His alternatives court madness, just as Beatrice's reconstruction of herself interfaced with incoherence and dysfunction. And madness is understood as a dissolution of self that, when it is a response to moral and political imperatives, revives a tradition of exemplary enthusiasm going back to Plato's dialogues, the *Ion* and *Phaedrus*. The skylark in Shelley's 'To A Skylark' (R&P 226–9) of June 1820 is perhaps his most famous figure for a discourse irresistibly beside itself:

Teach me half the gladness
  That thy brain must know,
Such harmonious madness
  From my lips would flow
The world should listen then – as I am listening now.

(ll. 101–5)

The inchoate quality of the bird's song results from its untimeliness. Early on in the poem an image of anachrony elaborates the evaporation of the individual bird into a general significance:

Like a star of Heaven
  In the broad day-light
Thou art unseen, – but yet I hear thy shrill delight...

(ll. 18–20)

The next stanza makes clear that Venus, planet of love, is the star in question. Out of its normal sphere, at the wrong time, the orientating power of bird and star is felt most deeply. This prepares for the analogy with the poet, an unbiddable character whose love expands our ordinary sense of connectedness and relation.

> Like a Poet hidden
>   In the light of thought,
> Singing hymns unbidden,
>   Till the world is wrought
> To sympathy with hopes and fears it heeded not...
>
> (ll. 36–40).

Obscured by his intimacy with illumination – 'hidden/In the light of thought' – the poet cuts a paradoxical figure, momentarily centre-stage in the explanation of the skylark. The difficulty for the reader lies in the typically overflowing quality of the bird's song whose generosity eventually escapes comparison. The reader is led from sympathy with unselfishness into a confrontation with the inordinate, the exorbitant, the daemonic. Finally, all that is left for the poet to desire is ungroundedness:

> Better than all measures
>   Of delightful sound –
> Better than all treasures
>   That in books are found –
> Thy skill to poet were, thou Scorner of the ground!
>
> (ll. 96–100)

Arguably, Beatrice Cenci died for trying to live in untimely fashion, seeking to transvalue norms that remained obstinately in place. The skylark, or rather the poetic projection of *its* value, risks inanition. A comparable emptiness, 'the intense inane', is celebrated at the end of Act III of *Prometheus Unbound* as the target for progressive humanity. The convergence of this desideratum with vacuity and distraction that Shelley so provocatively and calculatedly invites expresses once more the fearful challenge of being unhistorical. In 'Julian and Maddalo' (R&P 112–27) and 'Epipsychidion' (R&P 371–88) he appears fascinated by the area of undecidability into which this ideal can lead.

'Julian and Maddalo' probably resulted from Shelley's visit in August 1818 to Venice to see Byron about the welfare of his and Claire Clairmont's daughter, Allegra. The outings on which these and other exchanges took place were commemorated when Shelley sent 'Julian and Maddalo: A Conversation' to Hunt a year later. The Preface teases the reader into identifying Maddalo with Byron and Julian with Shelley. Its narrator calls Maddalo proud, but then implies this judgement is makeshift. His pride does not lead him, as might have been expected, to hold others in contempt. In fact he is chivalrous, and good company. His sense of superiority stimulates a nihilistic 'ambition [that] preys upon itself for want of objects it considers worthy of exertion'. This has produced his 'intense apprehension of the nothingness of human life' (R&P 113). His desires are infinite, but uncontrolled. His ascendancy over other people, therefore, also exhibits a weakness of constitution. The ascription of pride grants him something magnificent while criticizing his lack of prudence or overall *virtù*. He is a failed Renaissance man, the incomplete revival of a classical creature, one whose personal organization is disrupted by his personal excellences. Julian is his mirror image, a man who privileges social over individual aspiration; but in so doing he appears a highly eccentric or individualized representative of democratic progress. 'Julian is rather serious', we are told, a bit of a prig. The third main character, the lovelorn Maniac, stands for or intensifies both departures from that classical harmony indicated by the poem's epigraph from Virgil's tenth eclogue:

> The meadows with fresh streams, the bees with thyme,
> The goats with the green leaves of budding Spring,
> Are saturated not – nor Love with tears.
>
> (R&P 112)

The eclogue satirizes the obsessive love of Gallus by itself making love an unexceptional member of a catalogue of other country pleasures. Yet, *omnia vincit Amor*; love threatens anyway to transfigure any scheme that calls it ordinary or sets it limits. Sympathy for the Maniac, as for the skylark, shows where sympathies can lead.

The company of these two, then three, men is held up by the narrator, Julian, as a perfect forum, a virtuous friendship. However, missing from the analysis of each man's characteristics and failings is the lover who has shaped his life. This must be significant. The easy conversational style of the verse itself, in the striking opening paragraph, appears markedly sociable and welcoming. It is capable of bringing together both high-mindedness and circumstantial detail. The landscape is free of moralizing, yet reflects the friendship of the two riders, Julian and Maddalo. The unconscious interaction of the elements reminds the two horsemen of the calculated oblivion of their own jaunt along the Lido. The aerial merriment of the waves conjures a Shakespearian spirit. Julian and Maddalo's interplay or Wordsworthian 'glee' (l. 30) differs from that of sea, wind, and land precisely in the moral quality of friendship; yet friendship takes its *beau idéal* from a natural animation that cannot feel it.

The 'better station' Maddalo then conducts Julian to in a gondola supposedly delivers a still finer view of the Alps than was gained on the ride. Maddalo's purpose, though, is to reorientate Julian so that he takes his bearings not from a sunset complicit with the architectural imagination and embodying again the Wordsworthian dialectic of the elements, but from a literal building, comparatively limited and tendentious in its symbolism of human life. The 'madhouse and its belfry tower' (l. 107) is, claims Maddalo, 'the emblem and the sign/Of what should be eternal and divine!' (ll. 121–2); it is an unstrung constitution in which soul, thoughts, desires, heart and memory combine to baffle rather than articulate a purpose.

Unlike Shelley's pessimism, Maddalo's rather rejoices in its Gothic frisson than uses it to express a sense of untimeliness. Perhaps Maddalo uses pessimism strategically in his debate with Julian. It provides the opportunity to liken Julian to a madman – 'one like you . . . ever talking in such sort/As you do' (ll. 195, 236–7). The madman suggests still direr consequences for Julian's utopian belief in the power of the human will to realize our ideas of love, beauty, and truth. The madman is the Wordsworthian solitary of those Venetian wastes. Maddalo's friendship for him, drawn by a gentility above the madman's present fortune, is a one-way affair. Julian describes the madman's passion as 'wrought from his own fervid heart', a self-preying he in turn finds analogous to Maddalo's pride (l. 283). But, while Maddalo finds the world wanting, the madman is overwhelmed by its inordinate demands. Maddalo is too discriminating to suffer its vulgarity, but the maniac's sensibility is unbearably extended by the worldly calls on his sympathies.

The madman has been crossed in love. Of the love, if that is what it was, that produced Maddalo's daughter we hear nothing. In both cases, perhaps, the incommunicability in love of essential personal experience has caused the misery rather than more conventional differences. Sympathies, whose extensive sounding of life's painful chain of necessity would appal and agonize the partner, are repressed. Censorship warps the relationship, makes it a lie, and, through its conspicuous dissimulations, provokes the uncomprehending partner to scorn and hate. Love, as we have seen it defined by Shelley, finds our authentic identity in the generosity with which we can imagine a lover's response to us. If you think the demands of such a response to you would tear the lover apart, then the generosity with which you imagine her gift of yourself may be noticeably tempered. This less than total commitment then slights the lover, makes her feel undervalued, attracts her contempt. Only in poetry, again following Shelley's theory, can everything be said; but when that ideal unconstrainedness *substitutes* for rather than drives real relationships, it speaks a kind of dissociation from the world, a madness. It is, the madman tells us, like marrying death instead. Death is the only rival that, in a confused passage, the madman can countenance.

> I must remove
> A veil from my pent mind. 'Tis torn aside!
> O, pallid as death's dedicated bride,
> Thou mockery which art sitting by my side,
> Am I not wan like thee? at the grave's call
> I haste, invited to thy wedding ball
> To greet the ghastly paramour, for whom
> Thou hast deserted me... and made the tomb
> Thy bridal bed... But I beside your feet
> Will lie and watch ye from my winding sheet –
> Thus... wide awake, though dead... yet stay, o stay!
>
> (ll. 382–92)

By the time literature savours this pathology again (Tennyson's *Maud* is an obvious comparison) the philosophical spirit of its excessive Gothicism has disappeared. Yet already in 'Julian and Maddalo' the madman's version of the failed affair exonerates him too obviously as a philosophical actor in a dispute that otherwise sounds highly personal. The madman sees himself, of course, as one

Who loved and pitied all things, and could moan
For woes which others hear not, and could see
The absent with the glance of phantasy,
And with the poor and trampled sit and weep,
Following the captive to his dungeon deep;
Me – who am as a nerve o'er which do creep
The else unfelt oppressions of this earth
And was to thee the flame upon thy hearth
When all beside was cold –

(ll. 444–52).

Importance here becomes importunacy: overstated, the poetics of sympathy become the madman's eccentricity, his loss of perspective, his failed sense of proportion. Instead of an invitation to universalize the individual's experience, 'love's work' (l. 464) has become an effort to overcome the other's repugnancy, a saving of appearances. The watching, listening Julian and Maddalo find their 'argument was quite forgot' – a concession to the madman's pathos, but also an admission that he is no more than that pathetic figure, no longer a material witness in their philosophical dispute over optimism and pessimism. In conversation afterwards, they lucidly recapitulate his dilemma and its significant ambiguity.

And we agreed his was some dreadful ill
Wrought on him boldly, yet unspeakable
By a dear friend; some deadly change in love
Of one vowed deeply which he dreamed not of;
For whose sake he, it seemed, had fixed a blot
Of falshood on his mind which flourished not
But in the light of all-beholding truth;
And having stamped this canker on his youth
She had abandoned him –

(ll. 525–33).

It is not clear if his compromise with 'all-beholding truth' is cause or effect of love gone wrong. Can one person ever acknowledge fully the claims of others upon him without disintegrating personally? The women instrumental in this self-reflection are never called to the bar to give their story, and so the answer is fudged. Indeed, the very traditional positioning of woman as muse or divine mediator makes her role unfairly vulnerable to any personal inflexion, discredited by any step down from the pedestal. When Shelley revisits this Dantean and Petrarchan tradition in 'Epipsychidion', he is less than happy with the result. At the end of 'Julian and Maddalo', Julian returns to Venice from his unspecified but evidently saving connections in London and meets the grown-up daughter of Maddalo, now 'Like one of Shakespeare's women' (l. 592), a woman, presumably, capable of taking the initiative and speaking for herself. And, yes, she does explain to Julian how the madman and his lover met again and why they parted. But, once more, the woman is silenced – 'I urged and questioned still, she told me how / All happened – but the cold world shall not know' (ll. 616–17). These last words of the poem preserve the female's role of ineffable muse and so the dilemma of the poem is repeated, not solved. Women are crucial to the conversation but excluded from it. To remember Shelley's growing alienation from Mary is only slightly useful here. More helpful is to recall that, in 'On Love', love's work in joining up the specific individual 'with every thing which exists' leaves the beloved as the conduit of every voice but her own (R. 473). Was the madman's problem an aberration which Julian, to think optimistically, might have alleviated by finding 'An entrance to the caverns of his mind' (l. 573)? Or was he a version of Maddalo's tragic impasse: someone not too good for this world but exemplifying that to be good enough for it, nervously attuned to its miseries, destroys the personality and renders it incapable of relationship?

As in 'Julian and Maddalo', the personal circumstances of the relationship sketched in 'Epipsychidion' are displaced by the philosophical speculation of which it is the vehicle. To press for more detail, we are told, would be vulgar. Clearly we will want to belong to that 'certain class of readers' who can recognize the parallel with Dante's *Vita nuova* and so grasp the misguidedness of questioning the real basis of the exotic exaggerations of 'Epispsychidion' (R&P 373). However, lacking the religious foundation of Dante's symbolic extension of Beatrice, Shelley's Emily does seem to finesse a personal dilemma. The poem tries to make unworthy, by definition, Mary's discomfort from December 1820 onwards at Percy's frequent visits and letters to Emilia Viviani, imprisoned by her father, the Governor of Pisa, pending a suitable marriage. Shelley's criticism of his idealistic speaker is carried in the hyperbolic tone into which the secular reduction of Dante's sacramental love translates, 'Veiling beneath that radiant form of Woman / All that is insupportable in thee / Of light, and love, and immortality!' (ll. 22–4). The poem endorses, although *faute de mieux*, the sensuousness that remains, celebrating Emily's limbs, lips, eyes, cheeks, fingers, dress, hair, for the narrator still wants her as a metaphor, a means of making sense of a universal love free of personal interest. We readers are thus asked to enjoy a failed sublimation of erotic attraction, to take pleasure in the residual sexuality of a language untransformed by religious purpose. Of course one can say that this shortcoming is precisely the poem's plot and its verdict on the narrator. He aspires to move beyond personal desire for Emily, who provides instead a mirror for the soul's universal affinities:

I know
That Love makes all things equal: I have heard
By mine own heart this joyous truth averred:
The spirit of the worm beneath the sod
In love and worship, blends itself with God.

(ll. 125–9)

When Blake concludes in his prophetic book *Thel* that 'Everything that lives is holy', he also shows the cost of such sincerity. The difficulty with Shelley's version of the doctrine is that it neglects the economy of relationships it is considerate to observe with other people who cannot perhaps live with such broad-mindedness. Their suffering from the other's promiscuity suggests the actual narrow-mindedness that often lies behind such apparent emotional latitude and liberality. The narrator risks sounding self-serving when he congratulates himself on his advanced views and their superiority to the 'modern morals' of 'poor slaves' (ll. 154–5).

Again, this is calculated satire to some extent. It could almost echo a send-up of Romantic self-deception in Peacock's *Nightmare Abbey* or *Crotchet Castle*. But the trouble is that the idealism pitied in the narrator seems little different from the literariness excusing Shelley's own failure to find a contemporary form for Dante's universal vision. Shelley will try to do so right up to his last poem, 'The Triumph of Life'. In 'Epipsychidion', though, he seems liable to the *gran vergogna*, the great disgrace, which the

Preface quotes Dante attributing to rhetoric ungrounded in truth (R&P 373). Shelley's historicizing of the style of the *La Vita Nuova* certainly asks us to consider whether his disinheritance from Dante's religious faith gains sufficient aesthetic recompense. One could not justifiably omit the poem from any representative collection of Shelley's verse. Yet 'this soul out of my soul' (l. 238) generated by the flawed narrator dismisses, rather than confronts and works through, recognizable crises in relationships on the way to its symbolic climax. Can we read Shelley's distancing of Emilia, Mary, and Claire Clairmont in images of sun, moon, and comet as both the culpable idealizing of his narrator and the universalizing significance that he wants the women in his life to participate in by overcoming their characteristic antagonisms to himself and each other? Only by a highly questionable division is the tension that tore apart the madman in 'Julian and Maddalo' avoided.

Shelley's 'The Sensitive-Plant' (R&P 210–19), although written in March 1820, before 'Epipsychidion', frames the work assigned to love more ambitiously and abstractly. Another comparison with Blake, this time his Song of Experience, 'A Poison Tree', gets closer to Shelley's poetic parable. Blake's little poem invades the mindset of the God of *Genesis*. Its terse satire implies that only a psychopath would contrive the scene of instruction where Adam and Eve are thrown out of Paradise for eating the forbidden fruit. Shelley's much longer description of the Garden of Eden is at odds with the Bible's failure to accept openly the biological consequences of having a horticultural image of Paradise. For Blake, the world of Generation was an unremitting, deadening cycle to be transcended by the imaginative projection of ourselves out of its clutches into the dimension of eternity – a sphere circularly defined by just this imaginary flight. For Shelley, the supreme exercise of imagination is to sympathize with the material origins usually thought to extinguish it. So, while Shelley's plant echoes Plato's account of love in *The Symposium*, and 'desires what it has not – the beautiful!' (l. 77), this sensitivity remains vegetable. It destroys the opposition between ideal and physical aspirations. Precepts of French materialism and Romantic philosophy suddenly merge, and it is in its unconscious production of consciousness that nature maintains its enduring affinity with our essential self.

In Part the First of 'The Sensitive-Plant', consciousness is imaged as a 'light sand' at the turning-point of impression into expression.

And the beasts, and the birds, and the insects were drowned
In an ocean of dreams without a sound
Whose waves never mark, though they ever impress
The light sand which paves it – Consciousness.

(Only over head the sweet nightingale
Ever sang more sweet as the day might fail,
And snatches of its Elysian chant
Were mixed with the dreams of the Sensitive-plant).

(I. 102–9)

The poem's ending tries to counter the tradition that the poetic voice represented by the nightingale intensifies and is more valued as personal extinction looms. Keats's 'Ode to A Nightingale' moves from the celebration of an individual song to that of the species; from extolling the music of a particular bird to telling the history of its song, imagining in the process the common human nature identified by audiences to its perennial attractiveness. The sensitive-plant, an annual, does not have the option of becoming perennial, so the possibility of this larger self-expression must remain deliberately obscure, as it is for human beings, in excess of our individual powers of perception.

On the way to such paradoxical comfort, we encounter Shelley's explanation of the God of paradise.

There was a Power in this sweet place,
An Eve in this Eden; a ruling grace
Which to the flowers did they waken or dream
Was as God is to the starry scheme.

(II. 1–4)

Crucially, this feminized God-figure is also mortal. On her death, the garden rots in sympathy like a Gothic corpse.

The garden once fair became cold and foul
Like the corpse of her who had been its soul,
Which at first was lovely as if in sleep,
Then slowly changed, till it grew a heap
To make men tremble who never weep.

(III. 17–21)

The shocking physicality of a soul falsely thought immaterial is represented in the foetid growth of weeds and parasites. And that, the poem suggests, is one way of looking at things: personal loss can be such as to render the energies outgrowing it horrific and morbid. The Conclusion tentatively tries to rehabilitate the suspension of physical and mental difference, ' a modest creed', situating our understandable horror at individual dissolution, but gently resisting the personal view of death limited by individual perception.

That garden sweet, that lady fair,
And all sweet shapes and odours there
In truth have never passed away –
'Tis we, 'tis ours, are changed – not they.

For love, and beauty, and delight
There is no death nor change: their might
Exceeds our organs – which endure
No light – being themselves obscure.

('Conclusion', 17–24)

Interpreted as describing a 'Fortunate Fall', most influentially for Shelley by Milton's *Paradise Lost*, the *Genesis* story had demanded expulsion from the Garden as the price charged for individuality and history. However much individualism is portrayed as disobedience, giving it up no longer seems a way of remaining human. Hence another myth, the Christian one, has to be created in which can be imagined a last judgement returning us to Paradise, but doing so by eternally distinguishing everyone from everyone else. In opposing Christianity, Shelley typically opposes this individualism with collectivism. It might equally be argued that his own social origins make such opposing of individualism so agonizing a political apostasy – dissolution 'in this Republic of odours and hues', a draft calls it (Webb, 405) – that he has to imagine it as a break with the fundamental, saving myth of the Christian culture he inherits.

9

Popular Songs

Shelley's conception of his own role as a political revolutionary continues to ally the visionary with the campaigner. In letters to Leigh Hunt of 1820, he sees his task as one of popularizing reform. His projects for 'a little volume of *popular songs*' and 'a standard book for the philosophical reformers politically considered' are intended to make radical ideas generally accessible, one in poetic, the other in theoretical language. 'I see you smile,' writes Shelley, anticipating Leigh Hunt's incredulity. In fact the prose *A Philosophical View of Reform* (Clark, 229–61) is judiciously temperate in comparison with the apocalyptic political transformation Shelley allows himself to set down for Hunt. 'The system of society as it exists at present must be overthrown from the foundations with all its superstructure of maxims & of forms before we shall find anything but disappointment in our intercourse with any but a few select spirits'. This Philippic has the slightly comical appearance of enlisting political followers in the fight for a better conversation and social life for the Shelleys. Shelley, though, has in mind the way religious communities can create in discursive practice values that to outsiders might appear otherworldly and superstitious, 'having a power of producing that [object] a belief in which is at once a prophecy & a cause – ' (*Letters*, ii. 191). If you can persuade people of progress, and so get them to speak your language, the battle is half won.

The '*popular songs*' are presumably meant to follow the same logic, their poetic infectiousness recruiting sympathizers otherwise put off by difficult or extreme ideas. 'The Mask of Anarchy' (R&P 301–11), like another candidate for the collection, the sonnet 'England in 1819' (R&P 311), ends in faith and exhortation; not fanciful success, but 'graves from which a glorious Phantom may/Burst, to illumine our tempestuous day' (ll. 13–14). This imaginative enlightenment of others through sacrificial death repeats the action of the radical poet as Shelley agonizes over it in his own case. He is popularising his own fate. He will do so again in *Adonais* (R&P 388–406), when, 'A phantom among men . . . [he] in another's fate now wept his own' (ll. 272, 300). There he elegizes the poet Keats, politically traduced by the Tory reviewers but triumphant in a poetry he made an idiom for everyone. In popular songs, though, Shelley democratically makes us all poets through the assumption that in reading his poems we realize their aspirations to inspire. The conclusion of 'The Mask of Anarchy' similarly evokes a change in heart as the only experience open to its sympathetic readers, whose new solidarity will replace the 'base company' (l. 359) of all who had endorsed the militia's action in suppressing Manchester working people's demonstration of 1819 at St Peter's Fields.

Although the collection of '*popular songs*' was never published, other contenders for inclusion select themselves through their deployment of the same transformational meanings. 'A New National Anthem' (H&M 574) happily proclaims 'God save the Queen!', but this queen is not a Hanoverian but 'Liberty', lately murdered but soon to be restored upon an 'eternal throne/Built in our hearts alone' (ll. 29–30). In other words, if we can escape the prejudice that sovereignty and monarchy are the same thing, we have revived an ancient liberty. Republicanism, for Shelley, means a political arrangement by which citizens are self-governing; a society in which personal virtue feeds directly into civic virtue. His 'Sonnet: To the Republic of Benevento' (R&P 311), therefore, extols a city state's rebellion against papal authority as an internal victory. 'Man who man would be,/Must rule the empire of himself' (ll. 10–11). Only in a republic can we find a man 'being himself alone' (l. 14). No doubt this is idealistic. Shelley is untroubled by the apparent exclusion of women from this republican citizenry. Earlier, in 'Lines Written among the Euganean Hills' (R&P 103–12), he had imagined the Italian cities rising against the monarchies to whom they had been parcelled out at the Congress of Vienna in 1815, and 'Twining memories of old time/With new virtues more sublime' (ll. 158–9). The memories are of those Italian republics that resisted imperial and papal hegemony in Dante's time, and, behind them, the example of the Greek city states. The 'more sublime' virtues of their modern followers would presumably remedy their deficiencies in the treatment of women and slaves.

Without these idealizing, transformative impulses, though, politics in 1819 provokes Shelley to descriptions of necrophilia or cannibalism imaging sterile relations with past and future. 'Lines Written during the Castlereagh Administration' (H&M 571–2) is an epithalamion, a marriage hymn to the union of the 'Oppressor' of Albion with the 'Ruin' and death he has caused (ll. 11, 24). The 'Song to the Men of England' (Webb, 202–3) pictures them living unrebelliously under this appropriation of their creative liberties and has them entering 'fair England' like corpses into a 'sepulchre' (ll. 31–2). And 'Similes for Two Political Characters of 1819' (H&M 573) casts Sidmouth and Castlereagh in a succession of bestial forms in order to explain how they could so unnaturally devour their fellow-citizens. Finally, the depredations practised by England's Home and Foreign secretaries join them sexually: 'Two crows perched on the murrained cattle,/Two vipers tangled into one' (ll. 19–20).

It is obvious why poems like these were not published until much later, although there were booksellers around brave enough to take the risk. In 1820, though, Shelley must have been tempted to try the idea on Hunt partly because of the revolutionary activity all around him in Europe. In January 1820 Spain's king, Ferdinand VII, was forced to recognize the liberal constitution of 1812, originally a condition of his restoration but subsequently suppressed. The same constitution provided a model for reforms demanded by the uprising in Naples of July in the same year. Portugal was in rebellion by August. Unrest spread to the South American colonies. Foreign Secretary Castlereagh managed to be reactionary on two fronts, washing his hands of European upheavals when monarchical principles were not threatened and recognizing rebellious Spanish colonies prepared to adopt monarchical constitutions. Shelley's enthusiasm for these repeated, if brief, challenges to the monarchist heritage of the Congress of Vienna was uninhibited. 'You know my passion for a republic, or anything which approaches it,' he had told Hunt in April (*Letters*, ii. 180).

In 1820 Shelley most forcefully expressed this passion in two odes, the 'Ode to Liberty' (R&P 229–36) and the 'Ode to Naples'

(H&M 616–20). The Pindaric rather than Horatian ode that Shelley's poems imitate is perhaps the most overtly inspirational of poetic forms. Its meaning is largely to celebrate an act analogous to the creative energies belonging to its own production. Pindar's odes praise athletic success, but through mythic parallels that immediately synthesize the poem's own kind of creativity with the surpassing act of prowess it commemorates. If successful, the ode will have translated its subject's aspiration into a match for the legendary heroism of ancient myth. Its generous treatment thus transcends individual interests by adding to a mythic resource available to everyone sharing Pindar's culture. In Pindar's time, this expansiveness helped the ode substantiate the Panhellenic ideal supposedly embodied in the athletic games in which occurred the great victories it celebrated. Shelley's use of this tradition comparably shows how he might have believed that even in his most erudite and visionary productions the poet might still intend a popular song.

The theme of Shelley's great odes is announced at the start of the first, the 'Ode to Liberty':

> A glorious people vibrated again
>   The lightning of the nations: Liberty
> From heart to heart, from tower to tower, o'er Spain,
>   Scattering contagious fire into the sky,
> Gleamed.
>
> (ll. 1–5)

As G. M. Matthews has explained, Shelley's volcanic imagery is based on contemporary beliefs in cyclical renewal through seismic activity. It also articulates Shelley's certainty that political resistance is contagious because it is progressive. Revolutions happen when the emancipatory potential, the 'Liberty' endemic in the present, is released. Shelley's ode anticipates ideas he expressed less than a year later in *A Defence of Poetry,* the cornerstone of which is the claim that to read poetically is to see the future in the present. The odes of 1820 repeatedly image this process as one shared by poetic and political departures. As in Pindar's odes, the power of poetic analogy, vitally metaphorical, renews the culture of aspiration rationalizing definitively human practices. The progress of liberty, as Shelley's ode recounts it, is still founded on a Greek ideal, but runs through successive Roman, Saxon, Italian, and

Protestant examples, the detour of the French Revolution and Napoleon's muddled exploitation of its new-won freedoms, to culminate in the Spanish revolt of 1820. Shelley's history of liberty focuses a process common to all forward-looking activities, whether scientific, political or poetical:

> And, like unfolded flowers beneath the sea,
> Like the man's thought dark in the infant's brain,
> Like aught that is which wraps what is to be,
> Art's deathless dreams lay veiled by many a vein
> Of Parian stone...
>
> (ll. 54–8)

In these lines, growth and maturity are produced as if, like Michaelangelo, a sculptor had unlocked the statue hidden within a block of marble. Equally, Shelley's repeated similes suggest, the sculptor's creativity should express how we experience our natural evolution, from the inside, as the surfacing of consciousness and reflection. Hence, also, Shelley's typical use of subaqueous imagery, a landscape glimpsed through the sea's looking-glass, to suggest an uncultivated future existing at a tantalizing remove. Shelley's thought reflects a paradox of Romantic aesthetics: the more poetry is justified as a specific discourse with its own standards of correctness, the more it is seen to personify what Coleridge called 'the agent of all human perception'. In Shelley's 'Ode to Liberty', poetry in the more restricted sense of, say, Thomas Gray's 'The Progress of Poesy', which also claimed to be a 'pindaric ode', has expanded to resemble rather that radical 'Genius' celebrated in Anna Barbauld's poem *Eighteen Hundred and Eleven* or the writings of Blake. The final stanza of Shelley's ode emphasizes once more the symbiotic relationship of poetic and political inspiration: as one declines, so does the other. Poetry finally drowns in the futuristic element of its libertarian visions as the revolutionary hopes of 1820 are shot down like 'a wild swan':

> My song, its pinions disarrayed of might,
> Drooped; o'er it closed the echoes far away
> Of the great voice which did its flight sustain,
> As waves which lately paved his watery way
> Hiss round a drowner's head in their tempestuous play.
>
> (ll. 281–5)

Shelley's other revolutionary ode of 1820, the 'Ode to Naples', could scarcely be more stylized in its imitation of Pindar. Its epodes, strophes, and antistrophes appear in numbered sequence. Yet its cause, too, is popular. Shelley wants the Greek past of the city to show through its present wherever possible, supplying an image of the ancient liberty it has momentarily recovered. In the 'Ode to Liberty', Athens figured as a subliminal ideal, which, if brought to consciousness, could renew different historical periods with its 'delight'. The 'Ode to Naples' begins 'within the City disinterred', nearby Pompeii; but Shelley's archaeology digs still deeper to release the prophetic voice, the 'oracular thunder' of Greek inspiration. His letter of January 1819 to Peacock detailing his own visit to Pompeii is charged with a passionate sense of this continuity:

> The day was radiant and warm. Every now & then we heard the subterranean thunder of Vesuvius; its distant deep peals seemed to shake the very air & light of day which interpenetrated our frames with the sullen and tremendous sound. This scene was what the Greeks beheld, (Pompeii you know was a Greek city). They lived in harmony with nature, & the interstices of their incomparable columns, were portals as it were to admit the spirit of beauty which animates this glorious universe to visit those whom it inspired. If such is Pompeii, what was Athens? (*Letters,* ii. 73)

The ode implies that the same enthusiasm has led Naples to rebel against Bourbon rule backed by Austrian tyranny. Shelley imagines Venice, Genoa, Milan, and Florence responding to the poetry of the Madrid revolution, 'Spain's thrilling paean!' (l. 102). Rome even becomes like one of the heroes of a Pindaric ode – 'An athlete stripped to run' (l. 122). But in this updated version he runs 'From a remoter station / For the high prize lost on Philippi's shore' (ll. 123–4), the 'high prize' being the republicanism, the Greek ideal that perished with Brutus' defeat in battle by Octavian and Mark Antony. Rome, imagined to be free, is no longer ruled by the priestly 'power' of the Papal States but by its people's natural 'admiration' for liberty. Decoded, then, the poem's erudition only reinforces the immediate appeal of revolutions to an enslaved populace.

Last and most ambitious in this line of poems waging *Kulturkampf* for popular causes is *Hellas* (R&P 406–40). This 1,100-line 'Lyrical Drama', 'short and Aeschylean', was written in response to the failed Greek uprising in Moldavia supported by a ferocious revolt in the Peloponnese. Retaliation in kind followed from the Turks, and major players in Europe such as Britain responded with predictable indifference to anything not affecting their studied maintenance of the balance of monarchic powers agreed at Vienna. *Hellas* was popular first of all in the obvious sense that it was timely. Shelley was eager to see its '*immediate* publication', on which, he told his publisher, its interest depended (*Letters*, ii. 365). In the poem's Preface, Shelley apologizes for this 'newspaper erudition' in recent events, but nevertheless concedes that these details form the poem's 'basis'. He is more at ease when defending the Greek cause as culturally foundational, inherently representative of the common interests of all. He wants *Hellas* to figure 'the final triumph of the Greek cause as a portion of the cause of civilization and social improvement' (R&P 408).

Shelley's Hellenism recalls the ethnocentrism of *Alastor* and *Laon and Cynthia*. *Hellas*, though, shares the inbuilt defence of Hellenism offered by its model, Aeschylus' comparably topical drama, *The Persae*. *The Persae* commemorates rather than celebrates the decisive defeat of the Persian emperor Xerxes and his host at Salamis, and predicts the culminating rout of the Persians at Plataea. There are no Greek characters, only Persians, and the Greek element lies instead in the generous treatment it accords to the defeated through a sympathetic power that has been the Greek hallmark throughout the play. *Hellas*, similarly, is set amongst Turks, not Greeks. Xerxes is described as descended from the hero Perseus. His genealogy recalls a mythic resource anterior to the contemporary differentiation of Greek from Persian. Current Persian woes are dramatized as stemming from Persian decline from that authoritative example. Perseus famously slew the petrifying Gorgon. By contrast, the Persian empire, as the ghost of Xerxes' father, Darius, describes it, cast the nations it defeated into monuments to the Persian kings who conquered them. Perseus was the product of Zeus' union with Danaë when he visited her in the form of a shower of gold. But this common divinity now enjoys a degenerate afterlife in the Persian desire for wealth. The ending of Shelley's *Hellas* perhaps tries to revive that common myth of origin with the hope that for all 'The golden years return'. Xerxes' invasive bridge across the Hellespont similarly debases and parodies what unifies Greek and Persian. Defeat for the Persians, the Chorus tells us, is victory for free speech against a censorious tyranny.

Manifestly, Shelley could happily go along with most of this. His critical, mythopoeic energies were less in demand than they had been for *Prometheus Unbound*. *The Persae* would confirm him in his unreflective confidence that, in the words of the Preface to *Hellas*, 'We are all Greeks – our laws, our literature, our religion, our arts have their root in Greece' (R&P 409). Trust in the historical permeability of Greek ideals is tormented, though, by what the poem has to say about temporality, about the persistence of the past in the present. The poem's embodiment of this historical knowledge is Ahasuerus, the wandering Jew, someone whose integrity through history is the curse of homelessness not the blessing of longevity. He is the one who can say authoritatively to the Turkish tyrant, Mahmoud: 'The Past/Now stands before thee like an Incarnation/Of the To-come' (ll. 852–4). He instructs us in the ways of mutability. Mutability uses our intellectual apprehension of how things change to assert its power over any stage of existence or any temporary authority we might want to privilege.

> Thought
> Alone, and its quick elements, Will, Passion,
> Reason, Imagination, cannot die;
> They are, what that which they regard, appears,
> The stuff whence mutability can weave
> All that it hath dominion o'er, worlds, worms,
> Empires and superstitions – what has thought
> To do with time or place or circumstance?
>
> (ll. 795–802)

Failure to make transience the paradoxical basis of our understanding of reality, failure to conceive of ourselves as constantly mutating out of our present identity, leaves us subject to 'wolfish Change', time the devourer (l. 872). As Shelley made Jupiter discover in *Prometheus Unbound*, time is illimitable. But not only reactionaries with power vested in the *status quo* are embarrassed by change. Time, like life, will always escape any character in which we want to cast it, because, as we have seen, it is not that kind of thing. Time is rather the precondition for there being any character at all. Life will always 'triumph', to anticipate the title of Shelley's appropriately incomplete final poem on the subject, if we try to objectify it. Yet to practise complete resignation in the face of these larger processes – life, time, mutability – effaces subjectivity altogether. In the poem printed with the first edition of *Hellas*, 'Written on Hearing the News of the Death of Napoleon' (R&P 440–1), Shelley distinguishes between those encompassing perspectives and something more personal. The poem represents the larger framework as the devouring 'Earth', for whom history is a carnivorous food chain – 'I feed on whom I fed' (l. 32). This description also describes Napoleon's later imperial career so aptly that the narrator wonders that one does not die with the other, 'Earth' with her son. The alternative is to resist this marriage of biological inevitability and Napoleonic *gloire* in order to remember what might have been, 'And weave', as Earth says, 'into his shame, which like the dead/Shrouds me, the hopes that from his glory fled' (ll. 39–40). In that imagined difference, personal responsibility survives.

At other times, Shelley tenaciously hangs on to a purely negative concept of self gained through willingness to give up all self-defining interests belonging to particular 'time or place or circumstance'. An unfinished lyric, 'Death' (H&M 622), holds that

All things that we love and cherish,
Like ourselves must fade and perish;
Such is our rude mortal lot –
Love itself would, did they not.

(ll. 12–15)

Through love we can imaginatively get on terms with the inevitability of personal extinction. Love shows how our defining activity can project our essential self beyond the limits of the individual to live through others. All very good in theory, but Shelley's poetry simultaneously testifies to the agony of the sacrifice; from Beatrice to Ahasuerus, the straits of untimely existence are on display. Possibly compressed within the little stanza just quoted is also an excuse for unfaithfulness. At any rate, the idea that we cannot help privileging moments of metaphysical, cultural, and political apprehension even as we undo that privilege, that we can grasp the permanent 'One' only through the ephemeral 'Many', or that we know the deep truth to be 'imageless' only through successive failures to image it, is the ironic premiss for most of Shelley's late poetry.

10

The Gift of Death

Shelley's elegy for John Keats, *Adonais* (R&P 388–406), is his most sustained attempt to imagine death for the greater good as initiation into a larger community. Personal extinction becomes canonization. Shelley's syncretic title combines at least two myths: the Greek one of the young shepherd who is loved by Love itself, the goddess Venus, and is killed by a boar; and the Egyptian fertility myth of the god sacrificed to ensure the fruitfulness of the following spring, in which form he is thought to return and be resurrected. Shelley's implausible attribution of Keats's death to the Tory reviewers lets him connect both myths with yet another one that figures his main dilemma – the myth of Actaeon, the hunter killed by his own hounds as punishment for gazing on the forbidden beauty of Diana. Keats's hounds become his thoughts, the poetry for which he was viciously calumniated. And the enduring excellence of that poetry becomes the enrichment of our common culture and language through which he survives.

The plot, though, leaves Keats's afterlife subject to the vagaries of future interpretations of his poetry. Shelley's own tendentious reading begins the process. To become your readers is to be victim of the whims of the reading public: 'grief itself be mortal', Shelley concedes (l. 184).

> All he had loved, and moulded into thought,
> From shape, and hue, and odour, and sweet sound,
> Lamented Adonais.
>
> (ll. 118–20)

But moulding into thought, it turns out, is the act of a Shelleyan poet of mutability, a materialist aware of the dynamism of reality: of the need to grasp its nature through an intellectual construction of its genesis and of its future not received passively in sensation –

while the one Spirit's plastic stress
Sweeps through the dull dense world, compelling there,
All new successions to the forms they wear.

(ll. 381–3)

Allusive tribute to Keats's infectious poetic idiom shades into a Shelleyan identification with the forces of his own dispersal.

He is made one with Nature: there is heard
His voice in all her music, from the moan
Of thunder, to the song of night's sweet bird;
He is a presence to be felt and known
In darkness and in light, from herb and stone,
Spreading itself where'er that Power may move
Which has withdrawn his being to its own;
Which wields the world with never wearied love,
Sustains it from beneath, and kindles it above.

(ll. 370–8)

This merging, this willed union of Adonis and Actaeon, is the desire driving the whole poem. The poet is killed by his own success, which is precisely to have his thoughts and language survive him and become common property. Keats's saving popularity is prefigured by the procession of grieving contemporary poets who pay their respects – Wordsworth, Byron, Tom Moore, Leigh Hunt. Central to this mourning group is, of course, the 'Actaeon-like' Shelley 'Who in another's fate now wept his own' (ll. 276, 300). The dead Keats's gift of himself as Shelley's poetic vehicle then sets the precedent for the less restricted self-expression he has made generally available. That he could only do so by being a great poet, and that his individuality still inflects our use of him, is the poem's dominant myth.

The use to which Shelley puts Keats is not as eccentric or self-serving as might initially appear. Great elegies traditionally show their protagonists profiting from the experience of mourning; they draw comfort from the impetus gained towards 'fresh woods and pastures new' by the experience of coping with a loss first felt as irredeemable. The occasion here has developed Shelley's skill in a Spenserian stanza airy but monumental, foregrounding images of soaring and illumination, lifting and light. The poem's haunted conclusion is esoteric and personal: 'I am borne darkly, fearfully, afar' (l. 492). But the role the poem has constructed for poets has still been in the service of popular song, the story of everyone.

Privately, though, Shelley despaired of gaining popularity. He sent a copy of *Adonais* to Joseph Severn, the man who had nursed the dying Keats. In the accompanying letter Shelley claimed to resemble Keats in the fact that despite 'his transcendant genius Keats never was nor ever will be a popular poet' (*Letters*, ii. 366). On the other hand, Shelley described *Adonais* to his publisher as 'the least imperfect of my compositions' and doubted 'if *that* Poem were born to an immortality of oblivion' (*Letters*, ii. 355, 365). The poem, after all, imaginatively outwits a dismissive readership, its unlimited future displacing, even gaining definition from, the neglect of contemporary audiences. In the spring of 1821, just before Keats's death, Shelley had also written *A Defence of Poetry*. His disputant, Peacock, also pleaded with Shelley in private letters to make his poetry more accessible: 'you never think of your audience', he complained (*Letters*, ii. 375 n.). Like *Adonais*, Shelley's *Defence* answers Peacock by redescribing his poetry's difficulties with contemporary audiences as its power to interest future audiences. But Shelley remained deeply depressed, and in a letter of 1821 envisaged even the argument of his *Defence* turning against him. 'The decision of the cause whether or no *I* am a poet is removed from the present time to the hour when our posterity shall assemble: but the court is a very severe one, & I fear that the verdict will be guilty death' (*Letters*, ii. 310). At the height of the revolutionary enthusiasm inspiring the popular songs of 1820, Shelley had also written 'The Witch of Atlas' (R&P 347–67), conjuring up a figure of effortless intervention for the better in human affairs. Such facility is true only to the theoretical possibilities of poetic invention. It appears only to compound the problem of situating Shelley's creativity in the quotidian world shared by everyone else. But, since the poem goes to some lengths to invite this disquiet, it gives the impression of manipulating our scepticism. Cute descriptions of the tools of the Witch's visionary trade deliberately cloy; the rhyme mimes Byronic ingenuity.

And there lay Visions swift and sweet and quaint,
  Each in its thin sheath like a chrysalis,
Some eager to burst forth, some weak and faint
  With the soft burthen of intensest bliss.

(ll. 161–4)

In contrast to this exquisiteness is the use of the Witch's extravagance as a marvellous device for tracing actual atmospherics.

These were tame pleasures – She would often climb
  The steepest ladder of the crudded rack
Up to some beaked cape of cloud sublime,
  And like Arion on the dolphin's back
Ride singing through the shoreless air. Ofttime
  Following the serpent lightning's winding track,
She ran upon the platforms of the wind
And laughed to hear the fireballs roar behind.

(ll. 481–8)

In the introductory verses to Mary, Shelley compares his Witch to Peter Bell, the figure in which he had satirized Wordsworth in *Peter Bell the Third* (R&P 321–47) written in October 1819. This new comedy, the concluding stanza implies, satirizes not poetic pedestrianism but poetic virtuosity – a poetic love become idolatry. Poetic generosity carried to extremes can only celebrate its own licence. Shelley knew this danger well; Byron's poetic insouciance perhaps makes *him* the satirical target here?

In the last, fourth Canto of *Childe Harold's Pilgrimage*, Byron's narrator declares that he will 'twine/My hopes of being remembered in my line/With my land's language' (IV. 76–8).[1] Shelley's own poetry shows him nervous of this translation of aristocratic into poetic carelessness: he does not possess Byron's sense of a superiority never compromised by the lowliness of its sympathies. Canto IV despises the critical pretensions of connoisseurship or polite commerce, and prefers to be 'Chain'd to the chariot of triumphal Art' (IV. 445). It is the vulgar, 'paltry jargon of the marble mart' to try to 'describe the undescribable' Venus de' Medici (IV. 448, 473). Byron's artistic nobility, incapable of imagining its own debasement, mocks the anxious language of the artistic professional classes. Shelley's poetry, on the other hand, wills a future democracy, or its own popularity, but agonizes over the dissolution of its own cultural privilege this entails, a privilege that, 'The Witch of Atlas' shows, is such a source of pleasure as well as of authority. Byron slums it with a will in *Don Juan*, the great poem unfinished at his death. All linguistic registers are insouciantly fitted to his portmanteau *ottava rima* stanza. Shelley was only shocked by Byron's sexual promiscuity when it crossed class lines. Conceptions both of the vulgar and their superiors would, no doubt, be tranformed in a juster political set-up, but Shelley patently believed that the main adjustments, culturally speaking, were called for below stairs rather than above.

As if to witness the final experiment on this translation of the accidents of life into eternity, the man into the poet, the Shelley circle gathered round Leghorn and the Gulf of Spezia in 1822 from February until Shelley's death by drowning in July. Percy, Mary, Claire, and their friends Jane and Edward Williams lived together in the Casa Magni on the shore of the bay, but resident in the area were also Byron, the adventurer, Edward Trelawny, and eventually Leigh Hunt and his family. Amid remote and magnificent Italian scenery, enjoyed to the full on expeditions by land and by sea, Shelley worked out his thinking about mutability on two fronts, the domestic and the universal. His estrangement from Mary and growing attraction to Jane were the subject of conversational poems meditating personal instabilities. They conducted not a moral but a psychological investigation into the transience of passionate attachment, its subsequent, apparently obligatory reorientation elsewhere, and the loss of self-confidence this movement engenders. Shelley's analytic verve, displayed in his rebuttal of the slanders and libels of Robert Southey and more prurient detractors, here employs a discriminating but light sureness of touch. This urbanity was perhaps the single achievement of 'The Witch of Atlas' and the Homeric 'Hymn to Mercury' (H&M 680–700). It is founded on the overheard informality, the eclogue style of 'Julian and Maddalo', but gains in assurance until, confident of releasing poetic satisfaction, the poet can offer us the simple plotting of the everyday and anecdotal as in the 'Letter to Maria Gisborne' (R&P 313–21) of July 1820 or 'The Aziola' (Webb, 298) of a year later. This usage is maintained throughout the personal negotiations of the 1822 poems to Jane Williams, 'The

Invitation' (R&P 443–4), 'The Recollection' (R&P 444), or 'With a Guitar to Jane' (R&P 449–51). Such poems present little self-justification in the Byronic manner, but show stoical tolerance of the pains of love's divisions, and occasionally knowing strategies for masking it. So, in 'To Jane: The Invitation':

> Reflexion, you may come tomorrow,
> Sit by the fireside with Sorrow –
> You, with the unpaid bill, Despair,
> You, tiresome verse-reciter Care,
> I will pay you in the grave,
> Death will listen to your stave.
>
> (ll. 33–8)

'Stave' is an old word for stanza or verse', its outmodedness a match for the inopportune, verbose 'Care'. The adequateness of the personifications here belies the traditional antagonism of abstraction and felt experience so beloved of many of Shelley's opponents from Hazlitt to Leavis.

To mould nature into thought with such intellectual poise is, Adonais-like, to make it real. *Adonais* celebrates 'the kings of thought', the poets who can produce this third dimension. 'The Triumph of Life' (R&P 453–70) records their failure, or rather the universal unmanageability of life when they forget the partiality of their representations of it. Then, their mastery – 'Signs of thought's empire over thought' (l. 211) – becomes a tyranny, as insecure and ripe for revolution as any of the other tyrannies Shelley's poetry deplores. On the other hand, Shelley's 'Life' can grow uncanny, becoming something which possesses and enthralls us like an alien being. Petrarch's *Trionfi*, his poem's most obvious models, describe the triumph of what we might resist (love, fame), emulate (chastity), or suffer (death, time, eternity). Shelley turns what we are into our conqueror.

In 'The Triumph of Life', we are reminded, as in much Romantic philosophy of the time, that life has produced both the subject and the object of experience. 'Mont Blanc' has already demonstrated that it is a later, questionable use of that division to confine life exclusively to one or other pole, as natural object or spiritual subject. For contemporary *Naturphilosophie*, poetry counters this limited grasp with images of life as natural subject and spiritual object. But for those who cannot accept Shelley's materialism, this surrender of subjective privilege appears monstrous and enslaving. On the vast canvas of 'The Triumph of Life', this disgruntled group appears to include most of the worthies of Western culture from Plato to Kant. Understandably, many readers have assumed the poem either to critique the universality of its own critique, or else to be utterly despairing of the human condition. It may, though, be studiedly nihilistic. In other words, the poem may not simply be claiming that Shelley has got it right and everyone else – 'The Wise,/The great, the unforgotten' (ll. 208–9) – has got it wrong and so is led in triumph. Getting it right may look very like getting it wrong. Realizing the relativity of one's knowledge and foundational cultural beliefs is not much different from *confessing* the same errors you are keen to *detect* in others. Judgement on those life triumphs over is pronounced by the poem's unreliable narrator, Rousseau. Readers who think the poem critiques its own project can fasten on the unsatisfactoriness of someone who, like Rousseau here, is 'overcome/By my own heart alone' (ll. 240–1), his own worst enemy. But Rousseau's degeneracy is initially presented through the uncanniness of his body, its reversion to a nature no longer integrated with his thought or expressive of his personality:

I turned and knew
(O Heaven have mercy on such wretchedness!)

That what I thought was an old root which grew
To stange distortion out of the hill side
Was indeed one of that deluded crew,

And that the grass which methought hung so wide
And white, was but his thin discoloured hair,
And that the holes it vainly sought to hide

Were or had been eyes.

(ll. 130–8)

Gothic send-ups of Wordsworthian solitaries aside, what is at stake here is a recurrent pattern of dissociation. '"All that is mortal of great Plato there/Expiates the joy and woe his master knew not"' (ll. 254–5). Everyone is 'Actor or victim in this wretchedness' (l. 306). The point is that, while the sundering of mind and body suggests culpable lack of self-knowledge, it is going to happen anyway unless we can somehow embrace the apparently mindless life in what remains after death as our own, as something we can have an interest in or sympathy for. Again, what is condemned still looks very like what we are left with after detecting the error. Hence the horrific honesty of the poem. This is what life looks like purified of all consoling ideologies, bleached of all selfish constructions, truly 'the white radiance of eternity' at the end of *Adonais*, a vision scarcely distinguishable from the extinction of all vision.

> 'I rose; and, bending at her sweet command,
> Touched with faint lips the cup she raised,
> And suddenly my brain became as sand
>
> 'Where the first wave had more than half erased
> The track of deer on desert Labrador,
> Whilst the fierce wolf from which they fled amazed
>
> Leaves his stamp visibly upon the shore
> Until the second bursts – so on my sight
> Burst a new Vision never seen before.
>
> (ll. 403–11)

It is this universal blankness of Rousseau's vision, though, that lets him see also the evil of temporizing alternatives. The poem's pessimistic materialism is closest to that of Shelley's contemporary, Giacomo Leopardi, who at that time was living on the other side of the Appenines in Recanati. Working in the same materialist tradition, Leopardi argued in notebooks written in the 1820s that 'reason is our most material faculty'. Like Shelley, ultimately, he attacked the self-servingness inherent in false ideas that we can master in knowledge the life forces that produce us. Free of those illusions, we can accept that 'the highest philosophy is useful because it frees us from philosophy'. Life's triumph is to reveal the badness of our definitions of it. Only in surrendering to what appears to annihilate us, foundering on what lies outside the map of the world drawn by vested interests and authorities, as in Leopardi's great poem *L'infinito*, can we discover what is good for us: 'The only good is nonbeing; the only really good thing is the thing that is *not*.'[2] This apocalyptic stance is the authentic one for the writer who is as cynical of his own as he is of any other authority, keen, as in Shelley's 'Mont Blanc', to evoke a 'Power' that 'dwells apart'. One of the great contemporary works of European literature from which Shelley frequently took his final bearings was Goethe's *Faust*. In a letter to John Gisborne of April 1822, he uses Faust to attack Wordsworth:

> Perhaps . . . we admirers of Faust are in the right road to Paradise. – Such a supposition is not more absurd, and is certainly less demoniacal than that of Wordsworth where he says –
>
> This earth,
> Which is the world of all of us, & where
> *We find our happiness or not at all*
>
> As if after sixty years of suffering here, we were to be roasted alive for sixty million more in Hell . . . (*Letters*, ii. 406–7)

Wordsworth is complacent about the world as presently constituted, in which only the privileged are happy; and he is unimaginative about alternatives to the world that, Shelley implies, he consigns to fundamentalist Christian theology. Better, suggests Shelley polemically, to nourish a Faustian scepticism of both, to over-reach; to think, at all costs, outside those partisan frameworks that are passed off as necessary to thought itself.

Shelley died the most professedly European of the English Romantic poets. His *Defence* of his art praises a continuity of effort running from the Greek and Roman classics through 'Dante . . . Petrarch . . . Ariosto, Tasso, Shakespeare, Spenser, Calderón, Rousseau, and the great writers of our own age' (R&P 497). His typically burgeoning metaphors escape invidious comparison with his native Shakespeare because they revive the Baroque involutions of Calderón. His visionary idiom too fluently renders Dante's tradition to feel threatened, as much English Romantic verse did, by the example of Milton. His final scepticism owes less to the Humean beginnings of his thought and more to a shared historical sensibility at the start of a hundred years ending in proletarian revolution. He declares his unstinted openness to change in the guise of an overpowering pessimism. The principled refusal to be content proclaims that nothing exists indisputably, forever tailored to our essential needs, not the world, not life, not time.

O World, O Life, O Time,
On whose last steps I climb,
Trembling at that where I had stood before –
When will return the glory of your prime?
No more, O never more!

(Webb, 305; ll. 1–5)

Even the fixtures of Destiny, given in the poem's first, eponymous line, are displaced by a love seeking greater satisfaction, and their ideological rather than permanent character is proposed. In other words, given the context of Shelley's late thought, this fragment does not simply regret a 'prime' now past; it disbelieves the very idea of a prime produced by the benevolent conspiracy of world, life, and time. To express this critique through pessimism or constitutional unhappiness, though, is to remain honest about entrapment within a framework Shelley, for all his radicalism, cannot quite step out of. The better life must, tragically, be imaged as death, or else as some daemonic in-between, the unconscious vision of *The Triumph of Life* or the invitation 'To Night' (Webb, 304).

Death will come when thou art dead,
Soon, too soon –
Sleep will come when thou art fled;
Of neither would I ask the boon
I ask of thee, belovèd Night –
Swift be thine approaching flight,
Come soon, soon!

(ll. 29–35)

Notes

CHAPTER 1. SOURCES OF THE SELF

1. See especially Hazlitt's notice for 'Shelley's Posthumous Poems', *Edinburgh Review* (July 1824), repr. in P. P. Howe (ed.), *The Complete Works of William Hazlitt* (21 vols.; London: J. M. Dent, 1930-4), xvi. 265–84.
2. Matthew Arnold, 'Byron', in *The Complete Prose Works of Matthew Arnold,* ed. R. W. Super (Ann Arbor: Univerity of Michigan Press, 1960), i. 237.
3. Karl Marx, 'The Communist Manifesto', in *Karl Marx: Selected Writings,* ed. David McLellan (Oxford: Oxford University Press, 1977), 221–48.
4. Walter Bagehot, *Literary Studies,* introduction by George Sampson (2 vols.; London: J. M. Dent & Sons), i. 110.
5. Nora Crook and Derek Guiton, *Shelley's Venomed Melody* (Cambridge: Cambridge University Press, 1986).
6. Leigh Hunt, *Lord Byron and Some of his Contemporaries with Recollections of the Author's Life, and of his Visit to Italy* (3 vols.; Paris: A. and W. Galignani, 1828), ii. 76.
7. This version of 'Ozymandias' follows the copy-text established by Kelvin Everest in '"Ozymandias": The Text in Time', in K. Everest (ed.), *Percy Bysshe Shelley, Bicentenary Essays* (Bury St Edmunds: Derek Brewer, 1992), 24–43.
8. Kelvin Everest explores the textual corruptions of 'Ozymandias' itself, and illuminates their significance for the sonnet's argument in '"Ozymandias": The Text in Time'.
9. For a comprehensive and influential reading of Shelley in terms of transference, see J. E. Hogle, *Shelley's Process: Radical Transference and the Development of his Major Works* (Oxford: Oxford University Press, 1988); Andrew Bennett's discussion is in 'Shelley in Posterity', in Betty T. Bennett and Stuart Curran (eds.), *Shelley: Poet and Legislator of the World* (Baltimore and London: Johns Hopkins University Press,

1996), 215–23. Bennett's monograph, *Keats, Narrative and Audience: The Posthumous Life of Writing* (Cambridge: Cambridge University Press, 1994), is also helpful here.

CHAPTER 2. THE POLITICS OF IMAGINED COMMUNITIES

1. Jean-Jacques Rousseau, *Émile, Or On Education*, introduction, translation, and notes by Allan Bloom (Harmondsworth: Penguin, 1979), 85; Baruch Spinoza, *Ethics, and On the Correction of the Understanding*, trans. Andrew Boyle (London: J. M. Dent & Co., 1970), pt. IV, app. 32, p. 197.
2. Rousseau, *Émile*, 91.
3. For an admirable full-length study of Shelley's poet-figures, see Tim Clark, *Embodying Revolution: The Figure of the Poet in Shelley* (Oxford: Oxford University Press, 1989).

CHAPTER 3. AGAINST THE SELF-IMAGES OF THE AGE

1. Donald Davie, 'Shelley's Urbanity', in Donald Davie, *Purity of Diction in English Verse* (London: Routledge & Kegan Paul, 1967).
2. See especially G. M. Matthews, 'A Volcano's Voice in Shelley's', *English Literary History*, 24 (1957), 191–228, and William Keach, *Shelley's Style* (London: Methuen, 1984).
3. Compare accounts by Nigel Leask in *British Romantic Writers and the East* (Cambridge: Cambridge University Press, 1992), 108–18, and Saree Makdisi in *Romantic Imperialism: Universal Empire and the Culture of Modernity* (Cambridge: Cambridge University Press, 1998), 137–53.
4. Augustine, *Concerning the City of God, Against the Pagans*, trans. Henry Bettenson with an Introduction by John O'Meara (Harmondsworth: Penguin, 1984), bk. XI, ch. 6, sect. 5.

CHAPTER 4. HYPER-REALITY

1. F. R. Leavis, *Revaluation: Tradition and Development in English Poetry* (Harmondsworth: Peregrine, 1967), 172.
2. Arkady Plotinsky, 'The Quantum Mechanical Shelley', in Betty T. Bennett and Stuart Curran (eds.), *Shelley: Poet and Legislator of the World* (Baltimore and London: Johns Hopkins University Press, 1996), 264–5.

3. For a good exposition of 'Mont Blanc' within the framework of the Kantian sublime, see Frances Ferguson, 'Shelley's *Mont Blanc*: What the Mountain Said', in Peter J. Kitson (ed.), *Coleridge, Keats and Shelley* (New Casebooks; London: Macmillan, 1996), 172–86.
4. Mary Shelley, *History of a Six Weeks' Tour*, in *Complete Works*, ed. Nora Crook *et al.* (9 vols.; London: William Pickering, 1997), viii. 14.
5. William Wordsworth, 'Conversations and Reminiscences', in *The Prose Works of William Wordsworth*, ed. A. B. Grossart (London, 1876), iii. 458–67.
6. F. R. Leavis, *The Living Principle: 'English' as a Discipline of Thought* (London: Chatto & Windus, 1975).
7. Isobel Armstrong, *Language as Living Form in Nineteenth-Century Poetry* (Brighton: Harvester Press, 1982), 117.
8. S. T. Coleridge, *Poems*, ed. John Beer (London: J. M. Dent, 1993), 377, ll. 83–5.

CHAPTER 5. EROS AND CIVILIZATION

1. Paul Dawson, *The Unacknowledged Legislator: Shelley and Politics* (Oxford: Oxford University Press, 1980), 68.
2. G. W. F. Hegel, *Lectures on the Philosophy of World History, Introduction: Reason in History*, trans. H. B. Nisbet (Cambridge: Cambridge University Press, 1975), 16.

CHAPTER 6. COMMUNICATIVE ACTION

1. For an instructively sceptical view of Shelley's poetic ambitions in *Prometheus Unbound* from the critic currently closest to Shelley's text, see Kelvin Everest, '"Mechanism of a kind yet unattempted": The Dramatic Action of *Prometheus Unbound*', in Peter J. Kitson (ed.), *Coleridge, Keats and Shelley* (New Casebooks; London: Macmillan, 1996), 186–201.
2. F. Nietzsche, *Beyond Good and Evil: Prelude to a Philosophy of the Future*, trans. W. Kaufmann (New York: Vintage Books, 1966), 64, para 49.
3. G. M. Matthews, *Shelley* (London: Longman, 1970), 17.
4. Aeschylus, *Prometheus Bound and Other Plays*, trans. with an introduction by Philip Vellacott (Harmondsworth: Penguin, 1961), 42.
5. J. E. Barcus (ed.), *Shelley: The Critical Heritage* (London: Routledge & Kegan Paul, 1975), 225.

CHAPTER 7. CASUISTRY

1. Paul Smith detects casuistry in Shelley's own opportunistic adaptation of a gruesome tale to provide ethical theory in 'Restless Casuistry: Shelley's Composition of *The Cenci*', *Keats Shelley Journal*, 13 (1964), 72–85; for the use of 'casuistry' to unravel not only *The Cenci* but Romantic historicism as a whole, see James Chandler, *England in 1819* (Chicago: University of Chicago Press, 1998), esp. 498–507.
2. G. E. Moore, *Principia ethica* (Cambridge: Cambridge University Press, 1903), 5.
3. Ibid.

CHAPTER 10. THE GIFT OF DEATH

1. References are to *Lord Byron, The Complete Poetical Works*, ed. Jerome J. McGann (Oxford: Oxford University Press, 1980), ii.
2. Giacomo Leopardi, *Zibaldone di pensieri*, ed. Anna Maria Moroni (2 vols.; Milan: Oscar Classici Mondadori, 1983), ii. 1095; *Zibaldone: A Selection*, trans. and intro. by Martha King and Daniela Bibi (New York: Peter Lang, 1992), 68, 172.

Select Bibliography

EDITIONS

The Complete Works of Percy Bysshe Shelley, ed. Roger Ingpen and Walter Edwin Peck (10 vols.; Julian Edition; London: Ernest Benn, 1926–30; repr. New York: Gordian Press, 1966). Still the best complete edition, although better versions of individual poems and pieces of prose are to be found in the newer more accessible editions I have used.

The Letters of Percy Bysshe Shelley, ed. F. L. Jones (2 vols.; Oxford: Oxford University Press, 1964).

Shelley's Prose: Or, The Trumpet of a Prophecy, ed. David L. Clark (Albuquerque, N. Mex.: University of New Mexico Press, 1966). Accessible and generally reliable collection giving an immediate sense of the range of Shelley's writings.

Shelley: Poetical Works, ed. Thomas Hutchinson, *A New Edition*, corrected by G. M. Matthews (London and New York: Oxford University Press, 1970).

The Complete Poetical Works of Percy Bysshe Shelley, ed. Neville Rogers (4 vols. planned, two published so far; Oxford: Oxford University Press, 1972–).

The Lyrics of Shelley, ed. Judith Chernaik (Cleveland, Oh.: The Press of Case Western Reserve University, 1972).

Shelley's Poetry and Prose, ed. Donald Reiman and Sharon B. Powers (New York and London: W. W. Norton & Co., 1977). Authoritative versions of selected poems and bits of prose. Contains the whole of *Prometheus Unbound, The Cenci, Peter Bell the Third*, and *Hellas*, and some critical interpretations.

The Poems of Shelley, ed. Geoffrey Matthews and Kelvin Everest (3 vols. planned, one published so far: *1804–17*; London and New York: Longman, 1989–). The emergent standard edition of Shelley's poems.

Percy Bysshe Shelley: Poems and Prose, ed. Timothy Webb, critical selection by George E. Donaldson (London: J. M. Dent, 1995). Usefully contains the different versions of 'Hymn' and 'Mont Blanc' and other poems not in Reiman and Powers, though not the long poems. Donaldson's survey of the critical heritage is very helpful.

The Prose Works of Percy Bysshe Shelley, ed. E. B. Murray and Timothy Webb (one volume published; Oxford: Oxford University Press, 1993–). Along with Matthews and Everest's edition of the poems, this should eventually supersede the Julian edition.

BIOGRAPHIES AND CONTEMPORARY WRITINGS

Barcus, J. E. (ed), *Shelley: The Critical Heritage* (London: Routledge & Kegan Paul, 1975).

Cameron, K. N., *The Young Shelley: Genesis of a Radical* (London and New York: Macmillan, 1950). This first volume sets standards for taking Shelley's radicalism seriously.

—— *Shelley: The Golden Years* (Cambridge, Mass.: Harvard University Press, 1974). Sequel to *The Young Shelley.*

—— and Reiman, Donald (eds.), *Shelley and his Circle 1773–1822.* An edition of the manuscripts in the Carl H. Pforzheimer Library (8 vols.; Cambridge Mass.: Harvard University Press, 1961–86). Contains essential biographical sources.

Chernaik, Judith, *Mab's Daughters, Shelley's Wives and Lovers: Their Own Story* (London: Macmillan, 1991). This novel, by a top Shelley scholar, is more convincing than the biographies about this period in Shelley's life (1815–16), and more honest about the pleasurable fictions involved in any such reconstruction.

Clairmont, Claire, *The Journals of Claire Clairmont* (Cambridge, Mass.: Harvard University Press, 1968). Mary Wollstonecraft Shelley's stepsister's recollections are interesting in their own right as well as highly suggestive about Shelley's family life.

Hogg, Thomas Jefferson, *Life of Percy Bysshe Shelley* (2 vols.; London, 1858). One of three accounts by contemporaries of Shelley all published in the same year. .

Holmes, Richard, *Shelley: The Pursuit* (London: Weidenfeld & Nicolson, 1974). The most approachable account, full of explanations, ideas, and biographical risks, although not unpredictable on the poems.

Hunt, Leigh, *Lord Byron and Some of his Contemporaries with Recollections of the Author's Life, and of his Visit to Italy* (3 vols., Paris: A. and W. Galignani, 1828).

O'Neil, Michael, *Percy Bysshe Shelley: A Literary Life* (London: Macmillan, 1989). Careful, judicious, sympathetic.

Peacock, Thomas Love, *Memoirs of Shelley* (London, 1858). Sympathetic and astutely critical.

Shelley, Mary, *The Letters of Mary Wollstonecraft Shelley*, ed. Betty T. Bennett (Baltimore and London: Johns Hopkins University Press, 1980–8).

—— *The Journals of Mary Shelley, 1814–44*, ed. Paula R. Feldman and Diana Scott-Kilvert (Oxford: Oxford University Press, 1987).

Trelawny, Edward J., *Recollections of the Last Days of Shelley and Byron* (London, 1858). Unreliable but fascinating account upon which Trelawney expanded liberally with increasing distance in time. There is a modern Penguin edition of the 1878 version, ed. David Wright (Harmondsworth: Penguin, 1973).

White, Newman Ivey, *Shelley* (2 vols.; London: Secker & Warburg, 1947). The most detailed.

SELECTED CRITICISM

Bagehot, Walter, 'Percy Bysshe Shelley' in *Literary Studies*, Introduction by George Sampson (London: J. M. Dent & Sons, 1911), vol. i. Unexpected support.

Bennett, Andrew, 'Shelley in Posterity', in Betty T. Bennett and Stuart Curran (eds.), *Shelley: Poet and Legislator of the World* (Baltimore and London: Johns Hopkins University Press, 1996), 215–23.

Bennett, Betty T., and Curran, Stuart (eds.), *Shelley: Poet and Legislator of the World* (Baltimore and London: Johns Hopkins University Press, 1996).

Bloom, Harold, *Shelley's Mythmaking* (New Haven: Yale University Press, 1959).

Chandler, James, *England in 1819* (Chicago: Chicago University Press, 1998).

Clark, Timothy, *Embodying Revolution: The Figure of the Poet in Shelley* (Oxford: Oxford University Press, 1989). Subtle exposition of a new and important critical orientation.

—— *The Theory of Inspiration: Composition as a Crisis of Subjectivity in Romantic and Post-Romantic Writing* (Manchester and New York: Manchester University Press, 1997). Contains a good chapter on Shelley's *Defence*, but the whole book is relevant.

—— and Hogle, Jerrold E., (eds.) *Evaluating Shelley* (Edinburgh: Edinburgh University Press, 1996).

Crook, Nora, and Guiton, Derek, *Shelley's Venomed Melody* (Cambridge: Cambridge University Press, 1986).

Curran, Stuart, *Shelley's* Cenci*: Scorpions Ringed with Fire* (Princeton: Princeton University Press, 1970).

—— *Shelley's Annus Mirabilis: The Maturing of an Epic Vision* (San Marino, Calif.: Huntingdon Library, 1975).

Davie, Donald, 'Shelley's Urbanity', in *Purity of Diction in English Verse* (London: Routledge & Kegan Paul, 1967), 133–60.

Dawson, P. M., *The Unacknowledged Legislator: Shelley and Politics* (Oxford: Oxford University Press, 1980).

de Man, Paul, 'Shelley Disfigured', in H. Bloom *et al.*, *Deconstruction and Criticism* (London: Routledge & Kegan Paul, 1979), 39–75. De Man's article has to be confronted, as do those by the other four authors, Bloom, Derrida, Hartman, and Hillis Miller.

Duff, David, *Romance and Revolution: Shelley and the Politics of a Genre* (Cambridge: Cambridge University Press, 1994). Wide-ranging, exemplary scholarship.

Ellis, Steve, *Dante and English Poetry: Shelley to T. S. Eliot* (Cambridge: Cambridge University Press, 1983).

Everest, Kelvin (ed.), *Shelley Revalued: Essays from the Gregynog Conference* (Leicester: Leicester University Press, 1983).

—— *Percy Bysshe Shelley, Bicentenary Essays* (Bury St Edmunds: Derek Brewer, 1992).

—— '"Mechanism of a kind yet unattempted": The Dramatic Action of *Prometheus Unbound*', in Peter Kitson, *Coleridge, Keats and Shelley* (New Casebooks; London: Macmillan, 1996), 186–202.

Ferguson, Frances, 'Shelley's *Mont Blanc*: What the Mountain Said', in Arden Reed (ed.), *Romanticism and Language* (London: Methuen, 1984), 202–14.

Foot, Paul, *Red Shelley* (London: Sidgwick & Jackson, 1980). Magnificent polemic.

Gelpi, Barbara Charlesworth, *Shelley's Goddess: Maternity, Language, Subjectivity* (New York: Oxford University Press, 1992). Innovative psychoanalytical and feminist study.

Hogle, Jerrold E., *Shelley's Process: Radical Transference and the Development of his Major Works* (New York: Oxford University Press, 1988). Exhaustive Post-structuralist reading.

Keach, William, *Shelley's Style* (New York and London: Methuen, 1984).

King-Hele, Desmond, *Shelley: His Thought and Work* (London: Macmillan, 1960). Good on Shelley's materialism.

Kitson, Peter (ed.), *Coleridge, Keats and Shelley* (New Casebooks; London: Macmillan, 1996).

Leask, Nigel, *British Romantic Writers and the East* (Cambridge: Cambridge University Press, 1992).

Leighton, Angela, *Shelley and the Sublime: An Interpretation of the Major Poems* (Cambridge: Cambridge University Press, 1984).

Matthews, G. M., *Shelley* (Writers and their Work; London: Longman, 1970). Small but ground-breaking study.

—— 'A Volcano's Voice in Shelley' in R. B. Woodings (ed.) *Shelley: Modern Judgements* (London: Macmillan, 1968), 162–196.

Morton, Timothy, *Shelley and the Revolution in Taste* (Cambridge: Cambridge University Press, 1994). Ground-breaking study that moves Shelley's vegetarianism into the intellectual centre he always thought it occupied.

Peacock, Thomas Love, 'The Four Ages of Poetry', in *Peacock's* Four Ages of Poetry, *Shelley's* Defence of Poetry, *Browning's* Essay on Shelley (Oxford: Basil Blackwell, 1972), 2–19. Useful collection of related texts.

Pirie, David, *Shelley* (Milton Keynes and Philadelphia: Open University Press, 1988).

Plotinsky, Arkady, 'The Quantum Mechanical Shelley', in Betty T. Bennett and Stuart Curran (eds.), *Shelley: Poet and Legislator of the World* (Baltimore and London: Johns Hopkins University Press, 1996), 263–73.

Smith, Paul, 'Restless Casuistry: Shelley's Composition of *The Cenci*', *Keats Shelley Journal*, 13 (1964), 72–85.

Wasserman, Earl, *Shelley: A Critical Reading* (Baltimore and London: Johns Hopkins University Press, 1971).

Webb, Timothy, *The Violet in the Crucible: Shelley and Translation* (Oxford: Oxford University Press, 1976).

—— *Shelley: A Voice Not Understood* (Manchester: Manchester University Press, 1977).

Weinberg, Alan M., *Shelley's Italian Experience* (London: Macmillan, 1991). Along with Ellis, Weinberg helps situate the Italian Shelley.

Woodings, R. B. (ed.) *Shelley: Modern Judgements* (London: Macmillan, 1968).

Index